SCANDINAVIAN STUDENTS ON AN AMERICAN CAMPUS

Scandinavian Students on an American Campus

by

WILLIAM H. SEWELL
OLUF M. DAVIDSEN

UNIVERSITY OF MINNESOTA PRESS
Minneapolis

Foreword

Visitors in foreign lands have always been agents of cultural contact and transmission. The increase in "exchange of persons," especially after World War II, has stimulated interest in the mechanisms and consequences of exchange, particularly in the United States where for several years the number of foreign students enrolled in institutions of higher education has exceeded 30,000. Also characteristic of the recent period has been the growth of organized programs of exchange supported by governments, foundations, and other organizations. Since such sponsored exchange has been undertaken with a variety of avowed objectives — ranging from the promotion of international friendship and understanding to the transmission of skills essential to programs of technical assistance and national development — questions have been raised about the effectiveness with which student exchanges have served these purposes. The need for evaluation of programs has been widely recognized, and several major attempts at evaluation have recently been undertaken. To provide adequate guidance for the improvement of programs, however, evaluation must be founded on an understanding of the determinants of effects on the foreign student. Such understanding has been insufficient because of the lack of substantial previous research on cross-cultural education.

In this setting the Social Science Research Council early in 1952 appointed a Committee on Cross-Cultural Education. In view of the divergence among specific aims of programs, and the dearth of empirical knowledge of the processes and effects of exchange, the role of this committee was considered to be distinct from program evaluation; the committee was to plan and stimulate research that might lead to better understanding of the complex process involved in cross-cultural education. Practical considerations led to concentration on present and former foreign students in United States universities. With this narrower focus, the committee hoped to select significant problems and to carry research on them far enough to establish provisional findings and to indicate promising areas for further examination.

Support for a three-year program with this purpose was granted to the council by the Carnegie Corporation of New York, the Ford Foundation, and the Rockefeller Foundation. The present monograph is one of several reports based on research in this program.

The principal studies sponsored by the committee fall into two groups. On the assumption that difference in cultural background is an important factor in determining the consequences of foreign educational experience, intensive studies of students from several countries of contrasting cultures were first undertaken, beginning in the fall of 1952. These studies relied primarily but not exclusively on prolonged personal interviews, and were particularly concerned with the relation of cultural background to the student's adjustment in the United States, and to his readjustment after return to his home country. Four studies in American universities were coordinated by M. Brewster Smith of the council staff. Complementary studies of returned students in their home countries were directed by Cora DuBois, then of the Institute of International Education. All these studies benefited from consultation with John Useem and Ruth Hill Useem, who were then about to undertake for the Hazen Foundation the research reported in their book *The Western-Educated Man in India* (New York: The Dryden Press, 1955.) The committee is grateful to them and to the Hazen Foundation for their willing and close cooperation with its efforts.

The second phase of the program comprised more systematic studies of problems and hypotheses identified in the committee's review of findings in the earlier series. Only a few of many challenging leads could be pursued in the second group of studies, carried on during 1954–55. Several apparently important determinants of differing outcomes of sojourn in the United States, particularly determinants of attitudes, were investigated in detail. Mutual relevance of the several projects was again encouraged by joint planning and by frequent communication among the project directors, under the general coordination of M. Brewster Smith.

The foregoing account may well suggest certain cautions to readers of the monographs based on the committee's studies. The early projects focused on nationality groups do give, as intended, a picture of some varieties of experience of foreign students. The small numbers of students that could be interviewed, however, and the lack of systematic sampling mean that generalizations about the frequency of different reactions and their determinants can be misleading. Arbitrary extension of conclusions to all foreign students or to foreign students in a particular situation would be most hazardous. A different reservation is in order with respect to the second group of studies. These were designed to throw light on particular relationships that seemed to be important in the outcome of study in the United States. But focusing on these relationships entailed the neglect of others perhaps equally important. Cross-cultural research, moreover, is still in the pioneering stage. Other compromises and limitations are made explicit by the authors of the respective monographs.

The research sponsored by the committee, it should be emphasized, was not designed to evaluate present exchange programs. Studies of a quite different sort would be required for that purpose. But the monographs inevitably call attention to difficulties and even individual "failures," in their exploration of processes and determinants of adjustment, learning, and attitude formation in cross-cultural experience. A hasty reader, especially if he measures success in terms of complete acceptance of the United States by visitors, may conclude that foreign student exchange is of questionable value. The committee's studies justify no such conclusion. It is hoped that administrators will find in the committee's work a basis for better understanding of cross-cultural education, for more informative efforts at evaluation, and for future decisions as to policy.

The dynamic leadership and wide-ranging interests of Wendell C. Bennett, the first chairman of the committee, played an important part in shaping its task. Both professionally and personally the committee suffered a great loss on his death in September 1953.

RALPH L. BEALS
Chairman, Committee on
Cross-Cultural Education

Acknowledgments

WE WISH especially to acknowledge the role of Richard T. Morris who was an original member of our research group. He helped to plan the preliminary phases of the study and contributed materially to the development of the interview guide and coding schemes used in the study. Although he left the group before the final analysis was begun, his contribution to our thinking is reflected throughout the study.

We are also grateful to the personnel of the other projects in this series for stimulating discussion and criticisms, particularly to Richard D. Lambert, University of Pennsylvania; John Bennett, Ohio State University; Ralph L. Beals, University of California at Los Angeles; and Franklin D. Scott, Northwestern University. We thank the Cross-Cultural Education Committee of the Social Science Research Council and the University of Wisconsin for sponsoring the study. We are grateful to M. Brewster Smith and Cora DuBois for their critical reading of an early draft of the manuscript.

We acknowledge our debt to Murray A. Straus, Archie O. Haller, and Masako Yamada who assisted in the statistical analysis and in other ways contributed to the project. Our colleagues, Einar Haugen, chairman of the Department of Scandinavian Studies, and E. E. Milligan, professor of English and Foreign Student Advisor at the University of Wisconsin, were helpful in numerous ways.

Finally, we wish to express our gratitude to the Norwegian, Danish, and Swedish students who were the subjects of this study. They gave generously of their time and were a delightful group to work with.

W. H. S. AND O. M. D.

ix

Table of Contents

SCANDINAVIAN STUDENTS ON AN
AMERICAN CAMPUS

The Background of the Study

Foreign study has an old and honored place in the history of education. Information about its evolution, goals, and methods is scattered throughout numerous sources. Guy S. Metraux [1] has brought together and summarized much historical evidence pertaining specifically to the development of cross-cultural education. Whereas earlier foreign study was largely independently planned and financed for purposes of individual advancement, a new trend toward organized exchanges and officially sponsored and financed study programs has emerged. International student exchange has come to be seen as a means for the promotion of good will and understanding among nations and as an important instrument in the formation of favorable political climates and improved social and economic conditions in many parts of the world.

The United States has led among the nations in employing cross-cultural education as a means to world understanding and as an instrument in the execution of foreign policy. Privately endowed foundations have joined with the government in making possible very extensive exchange programs.

An analysis of the stated goals of American-supported exchange programs for foreign students was made recently by the Committee on Educational Interchange Policy of the Institute of International Education. This analysis lists the following five objectives in order of descending frequency of mention: [2]

1. To promote international understanding and good will among the peoples of the world as a contribution to peace.

2. To develop friends and supporters for the United States by giving persons from other countries a better understanding of the life and culture of the United States.

3. To contribute to the economic, social, or political development of other countries.

4. To aid in the educational or professional development of outstanding individuals.

5. To advance knowledge throughout the world for the general welfare of mankind.

For the most part, these goals emphasize sociopolitical aims. Only one of them deals directly with the promotion of individual and professional development. Actually, the importance of the individual visiting student's purposes may easily be lost in the concern for the larger aims of sponsoring agencies.

The various goals which international student exchange seeks to accomplish are at present being pursued in this country alone by more than forty-seven thousand foreign students enrolled in a large number of American colleges and universities.

As one of the Cross-Cultural Education Committee's series of researches,[3] the present study is concerned with processes and consequences of the sojourn learning and adjustment on the part of forty students from Scandinavian countries who were enrolled in the University of Wisconsin during the period 1952–54.[4]

The reasons for selecting Scandinavian students for study were many, but three were most important. First, Scandinavian students long have been an important segment of the foreign student group in American universities. The flow has increased greatly in recent years, particularly since World War II. During the period in which this study was done, the annual total number of students from Norway, Sweden, and Denmark was approximately seven hundred.[5] Second, despite the fact that Scandinavian students tend to be found in a number of major universities rather than concentrated in a few, Wisconsin has traditionally attracted a sizable proportion of them. Actually, the Scandinavian student group constituted approximately ten per cent of the foreign student body at the university at the time the study was made; they were exceeded numerically only by Canadians and Indians. Third, and most important, it seemed strategic to study a group of foreign students whose educational backgrounds were different from, but whose cultural backgrounds were similar to those of American students. Most studies have focused on students from contrasting cultures — especially those from non-Western and less technologically advanced societies. The problems of adjustment and the attitudes of these students may be so greatly influenced by "cultural shock" and "national defensiveness" that the influence of other factors on the outcomes of their sojourn might well be obscured.

Theoretical Framework

No one would deny the value of determining the extent to which the aims of international student exchange are being accomplished and how these objectives could be better achieved. There are, however, various reasons why such a frontal attack on this problem is not yet feasible. It has already been seen that the stated objectives of cross-cultural education are typically very broad and unspecific and therefore do not readily lend themselves to evaluation. Perhaps largely for the same reason there is no well-established body of theory about cross-cultural educational processes available on the basis of which a set of meaningful hypotheses can be formulated and tested. In view of this, the first in the Cross-Cultural Education Committee's series of researches were planned primarily as explorations into the nature and processes of foreign student exchange.[6]

The Scandinavian student study rests on a broad theoretical base in terms of which attempts have been made to identify relevant variables in the students' personalities, home background, and sojourn experiences and adjustment — variables which might reasonably be expected to have a bearing on a number of subsequent traits referred to as outcome variables.

According to the theoretical scheme we adopted, the sojourner is assumed to be situated psychologically within and between two cultural systems. The individual who moves from one culture to another thus may be expected to bring with him a set of more or less well-established skills, characteristics, expectations, aspirations, habits, norms, and values: these include facility in the English language; past academic experiences; prior contacts with other cultures, including the United States; stated purposes of the sojourn; expectations about the host country and people; feelings of identification with the home country; habits relating to social interaction, manner in which friendships are established, and educational and religious practices; personality characteristics such as perception of self, degree of flexibility, and dependency on others.

This set of antecedent factors is manifested at both the personal and social-cultural levels. Its parts determine differential adjustment, perception, and affect, influencing the students' initial reactions and impressions as well as the kind and rate of change which occurs during the sojourn.

Once situated in the new culture, the person meets with a different set of expectations about himself, and different customs, norms, and values — ones typical of the host culture and its members. Among these are perceptions and expectations about the student and his home country, guidance and advice extended, evaluation of his academic background, social interaction patterns, religious practices, as well as the general university and community environment. These factors operate as a second set of determiners of subsequent adjustment and impressions.

These two sets of factors in large measure define the social-psychological situation in which the foreign student finds himself. The way in which he perceives, judges, and reacts to the sojourn environment is likely to be influenced markedly by how he sees and evaluates various aspects of the home culture.

Purposes of the Study

The theoretical scheme presented above was a guide for the research, suggesting what to inquire about and what to look for in the analysis of data. On the basis of this scheme the specific objectives of the study were formulated. They may be summarized as follows:

1. To obtain information about the academic and social adjustment and success of the visiting students.

2. To obtain information about the content and feeling tones of the visiting students' impressions of the United States as well as the changes in these impressions during the sojourn.

3. To examine the relation between factors in the individuals' background, intellectual and sociopolitical orientation, personality, and the sojourn situation which together or separately might have a bearing on the students' academic and social adjustment and success, satisfaction with the sojourn, and images and attitudes toward the United States.

4. To discover possible promising leads and hypotheses for further study.

5. On the basis of the findings, to make tentative suggestions for the guidance of student exchange.

The Sample

Data were collected during the period of 1952–54. Forty Scandinavian students were enrolled in the university, all of whom took part in the study: twenty-two came from Norway, eight from Sweden, and ten from Denmark. The Wisconsin group reflected the over-all composition, in national origin, of foreign students in the United States.[7]

The students represented a fairly wide age range — from 18 to 40 — although they cluster in three groups: twenty-three undergraduates in the 18–26 age range, fifteen graduate students in the 27–35 age range, and two special students who were 39 and 40 years old. Four were female. Twenty-one of the students were single throughout their stay, fourteen were married, and five were engaged. Of the married students, all but three had their wives with them for most of the stay. In most cases the wives worked in Madison to help finance their husbands' study. Four students married American nationals while here. Approximately a third of the group came from highly placed families, as indicated by their parents' occupations and income. The remaining two thirds, with the exception of one laborer's son, were from middle-class backgrounds. The majority came from large cities, but a sizable minority were from small towns. Only two had been reared on farms. In these characteristics the group closely represents the situation in their home countries, where university students have traditionally come from the higher status levels and from cities.

The academic records of the students before coming to the United States were generally excellent. Many came on scholarships which had been earned by academic achievement. More than half were in the upper quarter of secondary school students in their home countries. All of them had studied English extensively in the secondary schools and none had any great difficulty in using English in either his academic work or day-to-day activities in the United States. Many of them had traveled extensively, especially in Europe, and about a fourth had studied in other countries.

Their reasons for wishing to study in the United States varied considerably, but their objectives fell in two categories: desire to acquire (or increase) professional competence and technical skills and desire to learn more about America. Those who came for specialized professional training and to increase their technical skills were mainly enrolled in engineering and the natural sciences. Electrical engineering, chemical engineering, and aerodynamics were the principal specialties of the engineers. In these fields, in particular, the Scandinavians hold accomplishments in the United States in high regard. This is also true of selected natural science fields, especially chemistry and biochemistry in which the University of Wisconsin stands high. A few came to study commerce and economics because they planned to follow commercial

Table 1. Background Characteristics of the 40 Scandinavian Students

Characteristic	No.	Characteristic	No.
Nationality		English-language ability	
Norwegian	22	High	17
Swedish	8	Average	14
Danish	10	Low	9
Age		Academic status at enrollment	
18–22	15	Post-M.A. standing	5
23–28	14	M.A. standing	5
Over 28	11	B.A. standing	5
Sex		Undergraduate	25
Male	36	Field of study	
Female	4	Physical and biological sciences	10
Marital status		Engineering	9
Single	21	Law, commerce, journalism	5
Engaged	5	Social sciences, education	6
Married	14	Humanities	4
Residential background		General letters and science	6
Farm	2	Source of financial support	
Small town (under 5,000)	4	U.S. scholarship	15
Small city (5,000–50,000)	10	Home-country scholarship	9
Large city (50,000 up)	24	Family	6
Occupational background (father's occupation)		Self	10
Executive, fee professional	13	Financial support during sojourn	
Official, manager, proprietor	6	More than $2000 a year	10
Minister, teacher	8	$1200–$2000 a year	20
Farmer, small businessman	9	Less than $1200 a year	10
White-collar worker	3	Previous travel to other countries	
Laborer	1	Extensive	18
Academic success at home (percentile rank in secondary school)		Some	9
		Little or none	13
Top quartile	22	Previous contacts with U.S.	
Third quartile	15	Extensive	15
Second quartile	3	Some	11
Bottom quartile	0	Little	14
		Sojourn purpose	
		Technical-professional only	12
		Social-cultural only	10
		Both	18

careers at home. Many of the students with technical and professional objectives came on scholarships provided by organizations at home. Those whose primary purpose was to acquire more knowledge of the United States tended to pursue work in the liberal arts, especially the languages, history, labor relations, sociology, and journalism. Many of them were supported by scholarships, provided by American sources, which were designed to promote Scandinavian-American relations and better international relations generally.[8] Both groups merged in their common desire for foreign travel and the hope that their career opportunities would be enhanced by travel and study abroad. Further and more detailed information about the group studied is given in Table 1.

These forty Scandinavian students in a strict sense are not a sample but rather are the universe of eligible students on the campus during the time the research was being conducted. Generalizations drawn from the study are, of course, limited by this fact. However, the group in itself is an important one since it is one of the largest concentrations of Scandinavian students on any American campus. As has been shown it represents considerable diversity in terms of its composition by age, marital status, socioeconomic background, rural-urban origins, academic fields, and career orientations. Comparisons with data published by the Institute of International Education indicate also that the Wisconsin group is quite similar to the total body of Scandinavian students in America in respect to age, academic status, national origin, sources of financial support, length of sojourn, field of study, and other important characteristics.[9] While this does not remove the limitations referred to above, it indicates that the Scandinavian students on the Wisconsin campus are typical of the total group at least in these important respects. Thus, the findings of this study should be of importance as a source of fruitful hypotheses and leads which may be tested at other universities on students from the Scandinavian and other countries.

Procedures

The principal data of the study came from a series of personal interviews. The major reason for employing this method was that in an exploratory study of this kind, it is necessary to cover many aspects of the students' background, experiences, attitudes, and beliefs, the dimensions of which are not known in advance and probably could be charted only in relatively flexible interviews. On the basis of prior knowledge and experience with Scandinavian students, we believed also that it would be difficult to get information of the depth and variety required in any other way.

In order to provide for both flexibility and comprehensiveness, an interview guide was developed.[10] It was employed as a guide to the areas and topics to be covered during the interviews rather than as a set schedule of specific questions to be asked in an exactly predetermined order or form.

The guide, which is reproduced in its entirety as Appendix 1, was divided into four main sections: arrival experiences and impressions, background information, preconceptions, and subsequent experiences and impressions. Usually a session of an hour was devoted to each of the first three sections; the last section took somewhat longer, and parts of the last section were covered again at a later time. (Excerpts from actual interviews are given in Appendix 4.)

Each subject was reached personally and approached in his own language when his cooperation was first sought. He was told the purposes of the study and the procedures to be followed. Because of the many hours of interviewing necessary, every effort was made to schedule the interviews at times and in places convenient for the subjects. On the average, the interviewing took a total of five hours for each subject, with an average of nine months between the first and the last interviews.

The interviews were all recorded on a tape recorder and later transcribed. The transcriptions ranged from 50 to 235 double-spaced typed pages. (See Appendix 4 for a sample interview.) All of the interviews were conducted by the junior author, who was himself a graduate student from Denmark at the time he was doing the interviewing. The interviewing was done in English but in a few cases the students chose to speak at times in their native tongue when they found it difficult to express their exact thoughts in English. The students were aware that their responses were being recorded, but there was never any indication that they resented the presence of the recording equipment or that it inhibited their responses.

In general, the atmosphere in which the data were collected was such that the students felt free to give any information they were asked about or which they thought was pertinent. There appeared to be not the slightest reservation on the part of the subjects to express freely their opinions on any of the topics covered.

The general university and community setting, in combination with the interviewer's position as a member of the Scandinavian student group, offered a unique opportunity for observation of the subjects outside of the interview situation. By participating in the Scandinavian students' informal social gatherings, the interviewer was able to make cross-checks between reported and actual behavior, and to compare interview material with behavior exhibited in these informal surroundings. In order not to disturb rapport no notes were taken on the scene, but the observations were recorded as soon afterwards as possible. These notes were used in the interpretation of different kinds of behavior and in differentiating among the students on important behavior dimensions.

To get additional information especially on the students' academic adjustment and success, we sent a Teachers' Rating Form to the teacher of each course that the students had taken during their stay. The teachers rated the students on such attributes as classroom participation, responsibility in relation to academic work, general academic adjustment, rate of academic improvement, English language facility, sociability, academic performance, and mental ability. (The Teachers' Rating Form is shown in Appendix 2.)

A questionnaire was sent also to each student's adviser to get information about the kind and extent of advice sought by the students, as well as about their general academic adjustment. (This questionnaire is shown in Appendix 3.)

Finally, the grades earned by the Scandinavian students while here were obtained from university records.

Analysis of the Data

In order to organize the information contained in the typewritten interviews for ready comprehension and analysis, a coding scheme was developed. The material was coded in two ways. First, all responses pertaining to various preselected topics were marked for verbatim extraction and categorization according to subject matter and the period of time during the sojourn to which they pertained. In this manner, the students' impressions of, for example, American family life soon after their arrival in this country were brought together under one heading. The richness of the interview data was thus preserved and yet organized for easy reference.

Second, because one of the objectives of the research was to explore relations among characteristics in the students' background, sojourn experiences, and the outcome of their visit, certain material in the interviews was put into quantitative form. This was done by assigning a three-digit number to each pertinent response. The three digits represented time period, variable, and a rating, usually on a five-point scale. Summary ratings were computed when several responses were made.[11] These codes were transferred to punch cards for quantitative analysis. Numerous cross-tabulations were then made, on the basis of which thirty-three variables were selected for further analysis. These variables were selected according to their bearing on the theoretical and practical aims of the study. (A brief discussion of each of the selected variables is contained in Appendix 5.)

The data of the study form the basis for the chapters that follow. Chapter 2 is devoted to the academic experiences and adjustment of the students. Their social experiences and adjustment and their impressions of American life are detailed in Chapters 3 and 4. Chapter 5 presents an analysis of the relations of selected variables to the outcome of the sojourn. Chapter 6 presents a brief summary and a discussion of the practical and research implications of the study.

Academic Experiences and Adjustment

THE reactions of the Scandinavian students to their educational experiences in America can best be viewed against a background of certain important features of the educational system, practices, and traditions of Scandinavia and of the particular American university in which they studied.

Educational Background

The educational systems of the Scandinavian countries are all very much alike, reflecting the cultural homogeneity of the three nations. Education is publicly supported and great emphasis is placed on academic achievement. Nearly all students attend public schools. Private and parochial schools are few.

Although reforms of the school systems were undertaken after World War II, the training of the students who took part in this study was hardly affected by these recent changes. The educational system of which they were products provided for early selection of those who intended to go on to institutions of higher learning. At the end of the fifth year of elementary schooling, the students must choose between an academic and a nonacademic line. The nonacademic line is generally followed by those who eventually take up unskilled or semiskilled occupations or who intend subsequently to seek preparation in special schools or evening classes for the trades, clerical work, and the like. Most of the students in the sample followed the academic line leading to the *gymnasium*, which they entered around age sixteen. It is normally a three-year course of study emphasizing mathematics, physics, languages, history, geography, and other basic courses. There are practically no vocational or recreational subjects. The curriculum is rigidly prescribed and considerable homework is required. The academic year usually is forty weeks long with an average of thirty-six hours of instruction each week.[1] The student must pass periodic examinations to continue his academic training.

Graduation from a *gymnasium* and the right to enter a university are based on a comprehensive written and oral examination administered by local school officials and national examining committees. The competition for high grades is keen and in fields of study for which higher educational facilities are limited even some very able students do not gain admission.[2] Graduation from the *gymnasium* constitutes a significant milestone in the life of the student. It implies a degree of educational achievement for which there is no exact American equivalent. *Gymnasium* graduates may be compared with sophomores and often with beginning juniors in the better American universities. It should be pointed out, too, that *gymnasium* students tend to be drawn largely from the higher socioeconomic levels of Scandinavian society.[3] Specifically, they are much more likely than not to be the sons and daughters of professional people, high-ranking civil servants, ministers, and teachers, even though farmers and industrial workers comprise the large majority of the population. Thus, they constitute a rather small and highly selected intellectual and social elite.

Of those graduating from the *gymnasium* about half go on to higher studies. Continuation of study at a university marks a distinct break in educational experience. Instead of a fixed curriculum, compulsory attendance, written assignments, frequent competitive examinations, and rigid supervision, the students are now given great independence, with free choice of subjects, freedom to pursue their studies at their own pace and in their own way, no required attendance at lectures, no formal assignments, and examinations to be taken when they feel ready. A university student usually studies about three subjects for the first degree, concentrating more on one than on the other two. Usually he gives full attention to one subject for a year or more before taking examinations and passing on to the next subject. Advanced university work requires still further specialization, participation in seminars, qualifying examinations, research work leading to a thesis, and defense of the thesis, much the same as in the graduate schools of American universities, except that the student proceeds more independently, may attend fewer seminars and lectures, and is considerably less beset by bureaucratic requirements.

Relations between students and professors are usually cordial but traditionally quite formal in the Scandinavian universities. Professors have very high status in society at large and are often given public honors for their scholarly works and their contributions to public affairs. Within the university they are treated with considerable deference by both students and junior colleagues.

Campus life in the American sense is largely nonexistent in Scandinavian universities. The schools and even the departments of most of the universities are fairly independent of one another and are usually located at some distance from each other rather than on a unified campus. Dormitories are few and students usually rent rooms in private homes. Where dormitories do exist, it is not uncommon for both men and women to live in the same house, with no strict segregation. Students are not supervised by faculty or by special deans and, in general, the university does not attempt to regulate their behavior. Rather, university students are looked upon as mature adults, capable of living their own lives.

Students' leisure-time activities are much less highly organized than in American universities. There is usually one large student organization at each university which has primarily intellectual functions, but which also provides for a few social highlights during the academic year. Social fraternities and commercialized athletics do not exist and by and large the students' social activities and recreation are individually planned and pursued outside the university proper. These activities often take the form of bull-sessions, frequently leading to heated debates over controversial issues. Extended hiking and skiing trips into the hills and mountains are another typical form of recreation, reflecting the traditional Scandinavian fondness for nature and outdoor living. Inter-Scandinavian travel is facilitated by close cooperation among the student associations at the various universities as well as by special rates granted to students by certain facilities and institutions open to the public.

True to their Viking ancestry, Scandinavian students also yearn to travel to foreign lands. As peaceful learners rather than as pirate looters they seek intellectual broadening and improvement of their foreign language skills on summer visits to Great Britain and the continental countries. About half of the forty students who were covered by this study had traveled outside the Scandinavian countries before coming to the United States.

In summary, it is clear that the aims and methods of secondary and higher education in Scandinavia are very different from and in many respects almost opposite to those of the United States. The emphasis in American high school education on social development for the largest possible number of students is contrasted in Scandinavian secondary education with disciplined training and rigorous selection for higher education of a limited number of intellectually promising individuals. At the university level, on the other hand, the American system provides for relatively close supervision of undergraduate students and tends to have a number of routine requirements governing many aspects of academic and social life, whereas the Scandinavian system gives university students almost complete independence in their academic pursuits and certainly in their social life. The Scandinavian university students tend to be more intellectually oriented, more highly selected in terms of academic ability and achievement, and generally come from higher status backgrounds than American undergraduates. They see themselves as an educational elite in a society that places high valuation on academic achievement while American students tend to see education as a means to better employment opportunities in a society emphasizing social mobility.

The University and the Community

The University of Wisconsin is one of the large Midwestern state universities. Its full-time enrollment on the Madison campus at the time of the study was over 14,000 students, more than the total university enrollment in all universities in either Norway or Denmark and only 4,000 fewer than in all universities in Sweden. It consists of several schools and colleges including the Colleges of Letters and Science, Engineering, and Agriculture and the Schools of Law, Medicine, Nursing, Pharmacy, Commerce, Journalism, and Social Work. These in turn are separated into many departments. The Graduate School is one of the largest and most respected in the country and attracts many foreign scholars each year. Like most large American universities, the University of Wisconsin is a complex organization. Despite its attempts to conduct student relations in a friendly and personal manner, its bureaucratic structure inevitably results in a certain degree of standardization of procedures.

For many years the university has attracted a sizable number of students from other countries. At the time of this study, the total foreign-student body numbered approximately 400. Unlike some other large universities, the University of Wisconsin provides only limited special facilities for the assistance and guidance of its visiting foreign students. There is no formal orientation program specifically for them and they compete on a merit basis with American students for fellowships and scholarships. Official facilities are limited to special instruction in English, an emergency loan fund, and the services of a part-time foreign student adviser. These limited provisions are not the result of any lack of concern for foreign students, but rather reflect the conviction that students from abroad should be integrated into university life as equals rather than being singled out for special treatment.

The Student Union provides for occasional meetings of foreign-student groups, but its policy is to encourage their participation in its regular schedule of activities rather than to promote special programs for them. The International Club provides for some of their social and recreational needs through its regular meetings and activities and its reception held at the opening of the academic year. There is a small International House which provides accommodation for fifteen foreign and fifteen American male graduate students. The International Student Committee of the university YMCA facilitates meetings between the foreign student and the American community by sponsoring excursions and arranging for visits to American homes. There are, moreover, clubs for certain specific foreign groups including a Scandinavian Club, sponsored by the Department of Scandinavian Studies. This club is not only a departmental adjunct emphasizing academic interests but also provides social contacts for Scandinavian students and interested Americans.

The city of Madison, which is the state capital as well as the seat of the university, provides a friendly environment for foreign students. Its population of over 100,000 includes a proportionally large number of governmental, educational, and professional people. Most people live in single dwellings, and except for two small areas of substandard housing near the university there is nothing resembling a slum.

Madison is more cosmopolitan and offers a greater variety of cultural opportunities than many other cities of comparable size. Its population is among the best educated in the United States.[4] There are frequent plays, concerts, lectures, and art and scientific exhibits sponsored both by the university and by the community. The attitude of the community toward the university faculty, toward the students, and toward foreign students in particular is very friendly. It can be said that the foreign student in Madison finds himself in a liberal sociopolitical atmosphere in which he is accepted and welcomed.

This is particularly true of Scandinavian students. Madison is the center of a region of heavy Scandinavian settlement, and Scandinavian-Americans are highly respected in the community. Many of these people are now concerned with the preservation of the home culture and have organized lodges and societies to that end. Some Scandinavian students take part in the activities of three of these groups (the Sons of Norway, the Idun Lodge, and the Ygdrasil Literary Society). In short, Scandinavian students are perhaps the most well received group of foreign visitors on the campus.

Adjustment to Various Aspects of University Life

Although most of the Scandinavian students had considerable general knowledge about the United States before their arrival, their information about American university life was limited. Only three of the forty had attended formal orientation courses conducted at smaller eastern colleges. The others had picked up what they could learn through reading and talking to friends who had studied in the United States. However, none of them had very realistic ideas about such routine but important matters as housing, registration, the advisory system, or academic routine, including class attendance, examinations, grading, and the rules established to govern student conduct. Their expectations in these areas were based largely on their own experiences in the educational system at home and in some instances they were hesitant about conforming to the rules and regulations of the new institution.

Housing and supervision of student life. Before leaving their own countries many of the Scandinavian students had made arrangements for housing here. Twelve of the forty moved into dormitories, eight joined fraternities, and twenty rented rooms in private houses or apartments. The latter group expressed considerable surprise about the limited space and dingy furnishings characteristic of student housing here.

Moreover, the unfavorable rate of exchange of Scandinavian currency into dollars made the rent seem extremely high.

The expectations about dormitory living of the students who initially moved into dormitories were hardly realistic. Their reaction to the new living arrangement was almost immediately negative. The chief objection was to the noise, and they expressed much surprise at their American fellow dormitory dwellers' lack of distinction between work and recreation. One said:

The Americans in the dorm don't seem to realize that some students may want to work once in a while. They act like children the way they scream and yell in the halls, and they have their radios going full blast until late at night. I don't see how they can study with a radio blaring next to them.

The idea of having roommates was likewise new to them. With one exception, the Scandinavian students who at first lived in dormitories later moved out and found quarters in private houses or apartments where they could devote themselves more privately to their academic and personal pursuits. It should be emphasized that the new living quarters were scattered throughout the university community. There was never any serious attempt on the part of the Scandinavian students to establish a Scandinavian quarter.[5]

The same objections to excessive noise and lack of privacy were voiced by several of the students who lived in fraternity houses. But they all felt that these were minor disadvantages in comparison with the opportunities for developing close friendships and taking part in the many and varied social activities which their living arrangement afforded.

No other aspect of university life here was as frequently objected to as the regulation of social and moral behavior. The Scandinavian students were shocked to find that the university's supervision of students reached into roominghouse, dormitory, and fraternity house living as well as dating and moral behavior both on and off the campus. Their reactions to these regulations were especially unfavorable. The distinction between acceptable and unacceptable behavior seemed strange to them; and they objected strongly on the grounds that the interpretation was artificial, unnatural, dishonest, and false.

The University's attitude toward morality here is ridiculous! It's so artificial. Take the rules about when you have to be inside the dormitories at night — when people are old enough to go to college, you would think they should be old enough to decide when to go to bed. And then they give courses in marriage! I used to live in a mixed dorm at home, and I find their dormitory rules here very strange. They don't serve the purpose for which they were intended. Under the surface the moral standards are no higher here than elsewhere. The trouble is that American moral standards are double — premarital sex relations are very much frowned upon, but you just have to go to the entrance of one of the girls' dorms before closing hour at night and you'll see the most disgraceful display of petting, necking, and kissing and wrestling! To me this is all part of the same kind of behavior, and the distinction they make strikes me as being very dishonest and false.

A student who had dated several American co-eds had this to say:

You actually feel quite silly when you go out with a girl and you are chased from one place to another by the campus police. You finally end up sitting in a drug store or a well-lighted park with 2,000 people around! Young students in love are really checked up on here. They don't even give you a chance to prove that you are a decent fellow!

It is important to note that unfavorable reactions to supervision of students' social life are quite prevalent among American students as well, but it is likely that the Scandinavian students found the regulations especially degrading because they had come from a culture which considers students of university age sufficiently mature to require no special supervision.

Although their impressions of supervision on the American campus remained unfavorable throughout the stay, most of the Scandinavian students made acceptable adjustments to this novel situation. As already mentioned, the ones who at first lived in dormitories subsequently moved out and rented rooms or apartments where they were more independent of campus regulations. Others avoided supervision in ways learned from their American fellow students.

Academic routine. Nearly all of the forty arrived in the United States during the latter part of the summer in time to enroll in the university for the fall semester. When school began they joined with thousands of new and returning American and foreign students to go through the maze of forms, waiting lines, distribution points, medical examinations, and fee payment stations which constitute the registration system at a large university. It is hardly surprising that several of the newly arrived Scandinavian visitors felt absolutely lost in the turmoil and that they found the experience disagreeable. Many were pleasantly surprised, on the other hand, by the friendly helpfulness of their American fellow students.

For some of the Scandinavian students entering the university was further complicated by difficulties about proper placement in the academic system here. Five students felt that their past academic accomplishments had not been fairly evaluated in the transfer and that they were placed at a level below what they deserved. A few others had experiences which in one way or another threatened their own high evaluation of their past educational achievements. It is obvious from the interviews that the students' pride was hurt. One graduate student still smarting from his transfer experience had this to say on the day before he left for home:

I was not given the proper recognition for my previous work when I came. They rated my degree from home equal to a B.A. It was a disconcerting thing. They certainly take great pride in their own academic system here! Why, they put me almost on an undergraduate level!

Most of the Scandinavian students, however, felt that they entered the university at the level most beneficial to their own educational advancement. Even many of those who at first felt slighted came to feel less so when, in time, they were recognized by their professors for their high-grade work or as they became more familiar with the university's standards.

With the exception of seven students who pursued a general liberal arts curriculum, each student was assigned a professor in his own field of study to act as his academic adviser. Some of the students were dissatisfied with the attention they received from their advisers at the time of registration, when perhaps they needed information on questions assumed by the advisers to be routine. They felt that "the advice consists mostly of putting a signature on a study list." In the long run, however, the advising system worked out to almost everyone's satisfaction. Questionnaires filled out by the advisers (see Appendix 3) reveal that, as a group, the Scandinavian students sought advice only occasionally; were mostly in need of information pertaining to their academic program, research, and financial matters; and usually followed the advisers' suggestions. The advisers described them as an interested and serious group of students who were intellectually mature enough to pursue academic work independently.

While all foreign students on the campus are invited to go to the Foreign Student Advisor's Office for orientation and guidance, the seven Scandinavian students who were enrolled in the liberal arts had no other university adviser. Some of these students felt that they needed more advice about academic matters than they received. With one exception, none had previously attended a university and they were among the youngest of the entire group. Perhaps this added to their uncertainty about what to expect. However, any inadequacy of academic guidance for these students was made less serious by the fact that their purpose in coming here was not primarily academic. For this reason, some of them were not seriously concerned with their studies. This was reflected in the grades they earned and in their teachers' and advisers' evaluation of them as students.

Almost without exception the Scandinavian students were unfavorably impressed with the rigid academic routine of required courses, compulsory class attendance, day-to-day assignments, frequent examinations, and objective tests which characterize undergraduate instruction, and to some extent graduate education, at a large university. The reactions are exemplified by these remarks:

The university system here reminds me of secondary school. All these rules and regulations make you feel like a little kid! They don't trust you; they tell you exactly what to do. You would think that university students should be old enough to decide themselves if they want to go to classes or not. I really think this roll-calling in class is childish! Also, the way their examination system is set up, it cuts the student's time into small bits, it prevents him from thinking and pursuing knowledge; as a result, he learns for exams not for life. Students here are forced to study. The way they check on you — it isn't free. And this is supposed to be free and democratic America! All these rules are all right for high school students but not at the university level. Take for example the reports I have to hand in, they have to be on this kind of paper, that size, this color, and folded that way! It's ridiculous!

Strong feelings like these may be a natural reaction to a new situation, the norms of which are inconsistent with those formerly known. The students, especially those who had attended a university back home, found themselves in an academic environment which, by comparison, was considerably more rigid and which called for conformity to rules which they felt should apply to pre-university levels only. Submitting to this kind of supervision was like reverting to an academic stage which supposedly had already been passed.

Especially in the beginning of their stay, most of the visitors seemed to apply indiscriminately the home country norms to the new academic environment. For this reason their antagonism against the prescribed discipline here was particularly marked during the early part of their visit. Although the large majority of the students refused to alter their self-conception and their perception of university regulations, they later on made various kinds of adjustments. Some students, however, were unwilling to modify their behavior. Although several of them received excellent grades in their course work, the unwillingness of a few to adapt to local procedures is illustrated in an adviser's evaluation of one of them:

He was an intelligent person but a poor student. His poor performance was due to his indifferent attitude toward academic responsibilities. He failed to attend classes regularly and to get his assignments in on time, resulting in poor grades. On some occasions he tried to evade required courses.

Most of the Scandinavian students chose to recognize the new norms and to comply with them but at the same time stressing that "these rules may be necessary for American students because they are less mature, but I wouldn't do any differently if all this supervision wasn't there."

When they first came, the Scandinavian students were commonly of the opinion that "academic standards in the United States are lower than at home." Their first experiences in a university which in many of its practices and routines resembled secondary schools in Scandinavia tended to confirm this view. It is also possible that their perceptions were somewhat influenced by a need for self-enhancement in a new and strange situation. Some evidence of this is found in the fact that those holding the most negative views were the ones who had suffered a loss in professional or academic prestige in transferring into the university. (See Chapter 5.)

As time passed and as the students became better acquainted with the new system, and possibly accumulated a vested interest in their foreign education, their perceptions of academic standards changed. Graduate students in all fields felt that the standards at the university were high. Undergraduates in the pure and applied sciences were in general agreement that the training they were receiving was useful and practical and was put across well. One engineering student said:

The lectures are well organized. The teachers develop a point rapidly and then go on to something else. The education here is more efficient and more practical and up-to-date than at home. You learn what is necessary, and I think you become a better engineer here because you learn how to tackle the problems you will meet when you go out and start working. I'm still happy though for the fundamentals I learned at home.

Another said:

You know, before I came over here, the engineering students who had returned from the United States always told us how good an education you get in America. It's common practice because everyone wants to keep his own standards high. I'll do the same when I go back. The engineers trained back home may have read more physics and may be able to solve tougher mathematical problems than we over here, but as a whole, we are just as good engineers.

All in all, the preponderance of negative comments by the Scandinavians concerning academic routine at the university should not be interpreted as a generally unfavorable attitude toward their educational experiences here. Indeed, there were features of the host university which they found much superior to those at home. Except for what they termed excessive heating of the buildings, they were impressed by the physical plant, especially laboratory and library facilities. Numerous favorable comments were made, moreover, about the friendly informality of student-teacher relations at the American school. The students were perhaps more in agreement about this than about any other feature of academic life. One graduate student's comment illustrates the attitude of most of the visitors:

The professors I've had have been very good, and I have been very impressed by how easily the students talk to their teachers, even the most famous ones. The professors leave their doors open and you can just walk in. They really show a lot of interest in their students and spend a lot of time on them. I think this is a great advantage. It is something that seldom happens at home.

The Scandinavian visitors found the American pattern in this respect much to their liking. A large number of them included this feature of the American culture among the ones which they would like to see transferred back to their own countries.

Academic performance. In general, the Scandinavian students did well in their studies. On the basis of a grading system of 3 for A, 2 for B, and 1 for C, the grade-point average for the entire group of Scandinavian students was 2. Separated according to graduate and undergraduate levels, the students' grade-point averages were 2.59 and 1.72 respectively. The undergraduate grade-point average for all students enrolled in the University of Wisconsin during the academic year 1952–53 was 1.63.[6] Thus, it appears that the visiting undergraduate Scandinavian students did slightly better than their fellow students at the university as a whole. No figures are available on grade-point averages for graduate students during the period in which this study was carried out. However, for the first semester of 1948–49, the grade-point average for graduate foreign students, excluding Canadians, was 2.22. If this figure may be projected to the period of 1952–54, then the grade-point average of 2.59 for the Scandinavian graduate students compares very well indeed.

Table 2. Teachers' Ratings of Scandinavian Students on Various Characteristics

Characteristic	No. of Students				
	Very High	High	Average	Low	Very Low
English-language facility	4	12	21	3	0
Class participation	3	7	21	9	0
Academic adjustment	9	17	11	3	0
Class performance	4	17	12	7	0
Rate of academic improvement	4	19	13	3	1
Responsibility	9	17	10	4	0
Sociability	3	17	16	4	0
Mental ability	8	21	10	1	0

The academic record of the visiting Scandinavians is consistent with their teachers' opinions of them as students. This is evident from the high ratings they received on the Teachers' Rating Form, shown in Table 2. According to these ratings the students on the average were of high mental ability, they were responsible persons, their academic improvement was rapid, and they appeared to adjust easily to the educational system. In the written comments that often supplemented the ratings, most of the students were described as especially intelligent and mature and as having little or no difficulty in adjusting to the new environment. The following comments made by teachers and advisers are quite typical of their evaluation of the majority of the visiting undergraduate Scandinavian students:

This student is extremely resourceful and self-reliant. He is serious about his academic goals, and he appears to have no difficulty in adapting to the American campus scene. He has an excellent command of the English language, is well liked by everyone who knows him and inspiring to his instructors and classmates. He is one of the best students I have had in a long time.

His adjustment has been very satisfactory. He is a well-balanced person and his work has consistently been very good. His presence at this University has been a great benefit both to himself and to his American associates.

This student is a fine young man — self assured and ambitious. He has a pleasant personality and has had no academic adjustment difficulties whatsoever.

Several advanced graduate students who had come here primarily for research purposes were described in equally favorable terms:

This student has had no academic adjustment difficulties. He started research work immediately with no difficulty. Later on he passed an excellent oral examination for his advanced degree.

A diligent research scholar, conscientious, quiet, and unassuming. He gets along well with his associates and appears to have no adjustment difficulties of any consequence.

Some of the Scandinavian students who had come here primarily for nonacademic purposes were less concerned about school work, and, as a group, they performed less well both in terms of grades and in terms of their teachers' evaluations.

He did poor academic work largely because he was absent from classes a great deal. He did not seem to take much time either in preparing his homework. Socially he fitted in extremely well and he was a very friendly and pleasant person.

He did very poor academic work, mainly because of outside activities which interfered with his studies. He missed many classes. However, he seemed to adjust perfectly well to life on an American campus.

It is evident from the teachers' and advisers' comments that the Scandinavian students as a group adjusted well to the American university environment and that they were well liked, intelligent, and able.

The students' evaluation of their educational experience. During the final interview the Scandinavian students were asked to appraise their educational experiences and accomplishments here. Most of the evaluations were very favorable; however, in view of the differences in motivations, qualifications, and psychological make-up among the group, it could not be expected that they would all be equally well satisfied with their educational experiences. One extreme of the range is represented by the following statement:

I was never completely able to adapt myself to this system. First of all, I wasn't given the proper recognition for my work back home. Then I got tangled up in courses and credits and I had to go to classes and give reports and what not. I was never allowed to work on my own. As it is, I'm thoroughly dissatisfied with my educational experience. I'm even dissatisfied with myself. I feel like throwing all my work in the waste basket — scrap the whole thing!

On the basis of grades and teachers' ratings this student had done only average work. His adviser pointed out that "He knew what he wanted to do before he came and he has not had much resiliency nor has he been willing to explore alternatives." It was apparent that he could not objectively evaluate his academic experiences as he was asked to do in the interview. His ego-involvement was so great that his evaluation turned out to be a tirade against the university for its failure to recognize the accomplishments and potentialities he believed were his. This case strongly suggests that loss of status in the transfer may be an extremely important factor in academic adjustment, particularly when the student is highly ego-involved in his academic work. The experiences of a few other students support this observation.

The other extreme of the Scandinavian students' appraisal of their educational experiences is exemplified by a quotation from an interview with another student, who had made an especially fine record in his academic work while here:

I was perhaps a bit skeptical before I came. I didn't know what to expect, but I have been very pleasantly surprised. The teachers and research facilities are excellent. I've gotten a lot out of my stay here — much more than I expected. I'm very satisfied. I think I've learned a lot. My career opportunities have definitely been improved as a result of my stay here. It has been a wonderful experience in every way.

The evaluations by the rest of the Scandinavian students fell between the two extremes illustrated above. They were especially in agreement that the training they received in classrooms and laboratories had been useful and practical. They found the instruction stimulating because of the free interaction between students and professors. In addition, many of the advanced students felt that their association with American fellow graduate students had added immensely to the educational experience, both in specific knowledge and for broader social and intellectual reasons. The relationship between the American and Scandinavian graduate students was harmonious throughout and led to mutual respect and admiration. In all, there was probably no other group who were evaluated so favorably by the visitors as their American fellow graduate students.

Although it was difficult for the students to estimate the future effects of their foreign study experiences, most of them were quite confident that their career opportunities had been enhanced by the visit here. In the case of several, their academic and technical purposes might have been served equally well at home or in some other country. However, there was wide agreement among them that their stay at the university had been an exceedingly worthwhile experience nevertheless, and that it had broadened their outlook significantly. These gains, in combination with the increased technical competence and the numerous professional and other contacts they had made in the United States, most believed, had enhanced their future career opportunities at home.[7]

Conclusions. The Scandinavian students' reactions to academic and campus life were characterized by initial unfavorable impressions of educational standards at the undergraduate level and the close supervision of students, and occasional dissatisfaction with the university's evaluation of their own academic backgrounds. However, the adjustments the students made were in almost all cases successful and their subsequent impressions of American university education were quite favorable — especially in respect to relations between teachers and students and graduate training.

By and large, the Scandinavian students performed very well at the university, as evidenced by the high grades they earned and by their teachers' and advisers' favorable impressions of them as students and researchers. In their own estimation the foreign study experience was very satisfying, and most of the Scandinavian students were confident that their educational experience at the University of Wisconsin would have a favorable effect on their career opportunities at home.

Social Experiences and Adjustment

Many of the visiting Scandinavian students could well have satisfied their academic needs at universities elsewhere than in the United States. As long as the choice was theirs, however, there were several reasons why they were drawn to this country. The long tradition of friendly relations between the Scandinavian countries and America was important, especially at a time when memories of the last war were still fresh enough to discourage study at a German university. By the same token, the American war effort had but added esteem to the fascination which the United States has always held for young Scandinavians. Mere distance from home and the realization that this would probably be the only chance to visit the New World was another reason. The students were anxious indeed to satisfy their curiosity about this young and vigorous society which only recently had risen to world leadership and they were hopeful that their academic responsibilities would allow time for them to do so.

In their efforts to satisfy this curiosity, they were actually aiming at what has come to be regarded by many as an important goal of student exchange. Promotion of international understanding as a function of cross-cultural study is thought of by most as closely related to the foreign visitors' social activities during their stay, particularly their interaction with members of the host society and the images they gain of its major features.

It is therefore of interest to examine the nature and extent of the participation of this group of students in American life and to describe the patterns of social adjustment they developed while in the United States.

This is the subject of this chapter. Equally important and closely related to this is the matter of the Scandinavian students' impressions of various aspects of American culture and personality and the developmental trend in their attitudes. This is the topic of the chapter to follow.

Social Relations

Exposure to the same general university environment made the visiting Scandinavians' academic experiences similar. Hence their reactions showed considerable uniformity. In contrast, their social life in America differed widely. Unequal opportunities and diverse motivations resulted in variation in the extent of interaction with Americans. Within a matter of hours after arriving here, a few students had established social contacts with fellow Scandinavians which they maintained throughout their stay, thereby limiting their social interaction with Americans. Other students tended to avoid their countrymen and sought instead to cultivate Americans. The motivations behind these opposite kinds of behavior can be inferred from the following two quotations:

I spend almost all of my spare time with some of the other Scandinavian guys. You know, we have the same interests and outlooks, we understand each other better, and you don't get homesick so much that way. Also, you can get some of the most valuable advice on school and where to eat and things like that from the other Scandinavian students who were here before you came. That's what I'm going to tell the students who are preparing to come over here when I get home — to get in touch with some of the other Scandinavians here.

Quite a different orientation was voiced by another student:

I hardly see the other Scandinavians here. It isn't that I don't like them, but I figure that if I wanted to be with Scandinavians I might as well have stayed home. While I'm here, I want to get to know Americans as much as possible. I think there are some of the Scandinavians here who lose a lot because they stick together all the time. They should go out and join in some of all the activities that go on. When I go home, I'm going to recommend to those who are going over here that they join a fraternity if they can afford it. It's really a good way to get to know American students.

Especially in the case of Scandinavian students, their own wishes largely determined the extent of their participation in social activities and community affairs. Certainly the attitudes of the people in this university community gave them no reason to feel unwelcome.

Initial contacts and impressions. For the group as a whole, the early period of their stay was characterized by frequent social contacts with Americans, but the number and types of people encountered and the nature of the social settings varied greatly from student to student. Social interaction with Americans was limited for a few students to chats with their landlords or fellow students. During the first few weeks after arriving, other students were guests at large cocktail parties, dances, and coming-out parties attended by hundreds of people and conducted in the best tradition of prominent families in this country.

Despite these differences in social experiences, the Scandinavian students' early observations of American social interaction and friendship patterns were strikingly similar. Not only were their perceptions very much alike, but the developmental patterns of their reaction to these perceptions were quite similar.

At first the visiting Scandinavians were overwhelmed by the spontaneous friendliness and open hospitality of the American people.

I was really amazed from the first day! First of all, on the bus out here people were talking and laughing and joking although they were complete strangers. The first day I was here some Americans asked me out for supper. They were very, very, friendly; everybody called everybody else by his first name. Meeting people and getting introduced seemed much easier than at home. It's very nice! They accept you at once here, they don't wait to see what you are like, they aren't suspicious. They all seem very interested in you and ask you all kinds of questions. You feel at home right away. Their friendliness is really amazing. I've been thinking, it's funny, even with the thousands of students around here, they all seem to know each other, and they remember each other's names; even my name which is hard to pronounce they remember!

To be appreciated, these reactions must be viewed against the background of certain common features of Scandinavian social interaction patterns. As compared with the United States there is in Scandinavian social relations a sharper distinction between friends and acquaintances. Normally, mutual high regard and complete confidence typify the relations between the individual Scandinavian and his few carefully chosen friends. These friendships are likely to have been long in the making but they may well last for a lifetime. Beyond these, a Scandinavian may count as acquaintances a large number of persons whom he will treat with a degree of formality not likely to be known even among strangers in the United States.[1]

The newly arrived students were pleasantly surprised indeed to find themselves in a social atmosphere characterized by openness and interest — an atmosphere which seemed immediately to invite to close personal relations and friendships. To many of them it came as a pleasant contrast to the formality and cautiousness typical of introductory stages in Scandinavian social relations.

Subsequent experiences and impressions. After some weeks in this country, the Scandinavian students came to have fewer social contacts with Americans. The pressure of schoolwork doubtless had an influence, but by now the first enthusiasm for the warm and informal relationships seemed to be wearing off. Instead, the students began to express doubts about the sincerity of these friendships. While the superficial nature of American social behavior was appreciated by some students, the discovery of the seeming shallowness of social relations was unpleasant to most. In fact, the students as a whole were more in agreement about this characteristic than about any other of the topics covered during the interviews.

People are very hospitable and friendly here, but sometimes it seems almost too much. I'm not sure that it's as deep and hearty as you would think. I've noticed that when people ask you questions, they don't always listen to your answer. I'm beginning to think that all the informality and nice phrases are a sort of formality to cover up for the fact that people aren't really interested in each other. I think that may be the reason also why you always have to *do* something at a party — play games or something. If you don't, people just stand around and say a few standard phrases to each other and go on to the next person. Their social relations here seem very superficial. You can't get into any discussion of serious topics with Americans; they simply don't know how to carry on a discussion! There is no depth in it. They forget tomorrow what they said today. Americans like to have many friends or acquaintances, but they have no predetermined reasons for making friends. It's easy to meet people here and to get to know them on the surface, but I think it is very hard to become intimate friends with them. They're lonely, that's why they like to gather in big crowds like at football games. It's very strange; it isn't easy to get used to.

The reasons offered for this superficiality were several — excessive emphasis on practical or material matters, standardized thinking resulting from syndicated mass communication, fear of not being accepted by others in a highly competitive society if one showed deviant behavior.

The feeling that social relations in America were superficial was not always changed as a result of visits to American homes. The reciprocal satisfaction gained from these visits seemed to depend particularly on two things: the host's ability to refrain from thinking of his guest as a representative of some underdeveloped corner of the world who inevitably must feel lost and lonesome in the turmoil of a technologically advanced society; and the visitor's realization that the practices and beliefs of his homeland have not been ordained by heaven for the benefit of all mankind. The host's ability in this respect did not always measure up to the student's expectations. While his opinions about the Scandinavian countries and people were generally very favorable, he was often quite ignorant of present day conditions there. Since on such visits the students were being closely identified with their respective home countries, any display of such ignorance was likely to be an affront. The Scandinavian students' ears were sharply tuned to misinformation about technical advance. This may have been because many of them had a special interest in technology; perhaps also their sensitivity was more acute since technology is one of the few areas in which they actually considered their own countries to be behind the United States.

They were very nice people. They did everything to make it pleasant. Oh, of course, they asked first how I liked it here, and then they asked all kinds of questions about Norway. I don't think they know much about other countries. They asked some very peculiar questions. Mr. X. asked if we have dial telephones in Norway, and I had to tell him that my home town was the first in the world to have a dial-phone system. I don't think they learn much about other countries in school here. The other person who was there had actually come over here from Norway some 50 years ago. I swear he thought everything was like when he left. I didn't understand most of what he was talking about! They had a very nice kitchen in their home with all kinds of convenient facilities. It would be nice if these things could be more available to the common man at home. But they really didn't know much about the rest of the world. I almost think they had expected me to turn up in wooden shoes and with a stocking cap!

Reactions like this were typical, especially to first visits in American homes. However, in a few instances when these early visits were accompanied by some sort of shared activity of the host and his guest, such as seeing a play or movie or hearing a concert, the experience was less trying for the students. Certainly it should not be left unmentioned either that many of the visits eventually resulted in friendships between the American family and the Scandinavian visitors which lasted throughout the stay.

Another aspect of social relations in America which was difficult for the visiting students to understand was the great amount of emphasis placed on formally organized activities, especially those carried on during leisure time. Many believed that there was too little opportunity for individually planned and unorganized recreation. The problem was not the lack of facilities or opportunities to join organizations, but the students' own reluctance to having their free time organized and formalized.[2]

Things are always organized and prearranged here; everything has to be done through a club — then there is a committee and a chairman and a program and what have you. Somehow it takes the joy out of it. You can't go alone or with a friend, there is always a group and a program and you all do the same thing. It seems to me that you have to be a social animal to be able to spend your spare time in whatever activities you happen to like.

Later evaluations. While the students' perception of American social relations and interaction patterns remained relatively unaltered, it should be noted that their evaluations changed markedly during the sojourn. After several months here many of the students came to see much virtue in American social relations — especially informality and friendship patterns. This is illustrated by the following response to the question asked during the last interview: What features, if any, of the American culture would you like to see transferred back to your own country? (The features mentioned most frequently concerned human relations.)

Well, first of all, I don't think the difference between the two cultures is too great to begin with, but I think the relations between people — neighbors and friends and workers — is more easy here. For example, you don't have to have a formal invitation to go and visit other people. I would like to see more of that at home.

Another student who at first had been critical of the shallowness of American friendships had this to say:

I would want to take home some of the open-heartedness, the way you consider other people when you first meet them — as a friend. Back home we tend to be suspicious of people until we know them. Before,

I thought Americans were too sociable, they made friends without a predetermined reason for it. Now I look on it differently.

As time passed many of the students formed lasting friendships with American fellow students, professors, and townspeople. Some came to know American families whose homes they visited frequently. A number eventually became interested in the organized activities of the community and joined campus organizations, and a few even became officers in student organizations.

Thus, it can be seen that the reactions of the students to their experiences in social relations in the United States generally followed a sequence with the following stages: (1) very favorable impressions of American friendliness and hospitality during the first weeks of the sojourn when perhaps Americans were going out of their way to be kind to the visitors; (2) a reaction of disappointment and temporary withdrawal after several weeks when the students discovered that American friendliness and hospitality had a somewhat different meaning than similar behavior would have had at home; this disappointment resulted in the feeling that Americans were superficial in their social relations and could carry on best in formally organized groups; (3) favorable evaluations of social relations after the students had been here for several months and had more experience with their American fellow students and other Americans.

Social Adjustment Patterns

It is evident that significant changes occurred in the students' appraisal of American social interaction patterns. A corresponding change could be observed also in their social behavior. After the period of general withdrawal from interaction with Americans, the Scandinavian students worked out satisfactory adjustments to the social situation and, in general, the social adjustment difficulties they experienced were few and not severe.

The nature and extent of the students' adjustments varied considerably, depending upon numerous facts about their personal backgrounds and the particular situation confronting them during their stay. Careful study of the interview protocols suggests that the students all became more selective in their choice of associates and activities as time went on, and that a limited number of social relation patterns developed which characterized the different members of the Scandinavian group.[3]

One group of students subordinated themselves quickly and effectively to their social surroundings by erasing their outward Scandinavian characteristics and adopting typical campus manners in dress and speech. Getting to know this country and its people by actually taking part in American life was one of the most important reasons for their visit here. Throughout their stay these students were *enthusiastic participants* in numerous American formal and informal social activities both on and off the campus. Being well versed in the social graces and aided also by advice about local customs from American friends and fraternity brothers, the students in this group were able to adapt remarkably rapidly and well to the local social scene. Their social adjustment seemed more rapid than complete; but without exception they found American social life exciting and at least temporarily satisfying. Their ready adoption of American traits may have been a technique for gaining acceptance from their fellow students, but it probably established an effective social situation for learning about American life. Very likely, in the course of their sojourn, these students adopted certain traits which will not generally be approved at home, and their adjustment upon return may be made difficult by this. These students are likely to be strong advocates of American ideas in the home country.

Another group had little need or desire to involve themselves socially or emotionally with the United States. Their purposes in coming here were often limited in scope, technical, and well defined. Being anxious to reach these objectives as quickly as possible, they devoted much time to their academic pursuits. Although they did not deliberately avoid companionship with Americans, these students tended to satisfy their social needs among themselves; and while they did not attempt to exhibit their Scandinavian characteristics, they never seemed to lose their close identity with the home culture. In general, these visitors appeared to prefer to maintain the role of *detached observer* as far as social activities were concerned. Because of their limited participation in American life, they probably experienced fewer social adjustment problems here than any other group of the visitors. Their unique role perception was reflected in their attitudes toward American life, which, with the exception of attitudes toward university education, were noticeably neutral. For the most part they accepted things as they found them and were not perceptibly influenced by their contacts with Americans.

A third group was even more closely tied to the home culture, but they seemed to exhibit rather than disguise their national identity in speech, clothing, and mannerisms. In social situations with Americans they could often be observed to advocate many characteristics of the home culture as being especially desirable. Unlike the detached observers, they were eager to establish contact with the American community; but their social interaction with Americans was typically carried out through organizations and clubs or as a result of formal invitations to American homes. Very seldom did their social activities take the form of informal bull sessions and gatherings with Americans. Their contribution to cross-cultural exchange of ideas seemed to be mostly in the form of "promoting" or "selling" the home country. It seems likely that in their preoccupation with preaching to the host society, these *promoters* may to some extent have lost out in the matter of learning from it. However, because of their participation in at least certain kinds of social activities here, they are likely to be affected more markedly by the foreign experience than are the detached observers.

Finally, there were a few students, usually those who had been here a long time, who for various reasons were not especially attached to the home culture. In most cases their status at home was relatively low and some of them may well have viewed the foreign experience as a chance to explore opportunities elsewhere. These students all had become completely absorbed into the social-relations pattern of the host culture. Their social and recreational activities seemed to be motivated purely by the enjoyment these activities afforded, and they had established close relations with a number of Americans with whom they engaged in typical local forms of recreation — fishing, golfing, picnicking, and watching sports events. The social adjustment of this group of *settlers* seemed slower and more problematic than that of the enthusiastic participants, but their adaptation to American life was much more thorough and genuine. It is possible that some of the Scandinavian students who followed this pattern of adjustment may never return to their home country permanently. Those who do return are not likely to be so well satisfied as some of the other types, and some of them may return to this country later on.

These four adjustment types are by no means rigid categories, nor do they pretend to depict every possible pattern of adjustment. There were a few students whose style of adjustment is not covered by any of these types. But the four patterns emerged with sufficient clarity to indicate that students may develop a variety of adjustment patterns for coping adequately with new social situations. We hope that these types may be further tested in other studies to determine their generality for other groups of foreign students and other sojourn situations.

Conclusions

This analysis of the Scandinavian students' social experiences and adjustment in the United States indicates that (1) the visitors' social interaction was at first characterized by many contacts with Americans, followed by a period of less frequent association, and finally by increased interaction with selected American persons and groups. This behavior pattern was usually accompanied by initially favorable impressions of American friendliness and informality, which later turned to perceptions of superficiality and lack of genuineness in social relations here, which in turn became generally favorable reactions toward American social-relations norms; (2) the Scandinavian students' social adjustment was observed to take, in most cases, one of four distinct patterns, distinguishable in extent and nature of social activity — the *enthusiastic participants* whose behavior was characterized by outward assimilation and extensive interaction with Americans; the *detached observers* who involved themselves as little as possible with the host society; the *promoters* whose social contacts seemed motivated mainly by a desire to "sell" the home culture to Americans; and the *settlers* who, for various reasons, appeared to have cut their ties with the home country and were content in their relatively deep submergence in the new culture; (3) despite their temporary tendency to withdraw from American social life, the students did not seem to experience severe social adjustment difficulties. Although the various adjustment patterns would perhaps not all be considered completely desirable in terms of certain objectives of foreign student exchange, the students themselves were all satisfied with their social experiences in this country, and many of them eventually came to see much virtue in American social-relations practices.

CHAPTER

4

Impressions of American Culture and Personality

In the course of his first interview, the Scandinavian student was questioned about his preconceptions and arrival impressions of the host culture — his opinions of various American institutions and aspects of social structure. Part of each succeeding interview and much of the last interview was devoted to these same topics. This procedure was followed in order to get information about the content and affect as well as the developmental trend in the students' attitudes. Their impressions of family life, recreation, art, politics, economics, religion, social structure, and race relations were consistent enough to form patterns describable for the group of students as a whole. These patterns, the variation in them, and the developmental trends in the students' impressions are some of the most revealing and important findings of the research. In the following pages, the Scandinavian visitors' impressions of these various aspects of American culture will be described. This will be followed by a brief summary analysis of the trends in their general reactions to American life.

Family and Home Life

The Scandinavian students did not hesitate to express their dislike for those selected features of the new culture of which they did not approve, but it should not be inferred that their attitudes toward this country were generally unfavorable, nor that they were unappreciative of the friendly reception extended by the American community. Perhaps the best evidence of this is the marked change in their perceptions

39

of and attitudes toward American family life. Before they arrived, the students tended to view this aspect of American life with mild reservation and misgivings. They were dubious about child-rearing practices and frequently mentioned the high divorce rate as an indication of the American family's instability.

After some time here the mention of divorce dropped out almost entirely, and though most of the students felt that child-rearing practices were too liberal, they were favorably impressed with the easy and free relations between parents and children and with the spirit of cooperation with which young couples shared the household duties. These favorable impressions were tempered only by the observation that home life was being disrupted by too many outside influences. This feeling was very common but was especially marked among the students who came from rural Scandinavia, where family life is more patriarchal and autocratic, and where, in the absence of many commercial recreational facilities, family relations are comparatively close.

It's very nice to see the children talk freely to their parents and how the father takes an interest in the kids' games and hobbies. I don't think though that the average family is as close and unified as at home. The home isn't the center of activities; the children are off in all directions to all kinds of meetings and parties. You sometimes get the impression that the home is a place where the family comes to eat and sleep.

In essence, this observation fits into a familiar pattern in the students' images of American interpersonal relations — easy, free, and spontaneous interaction on the surface but with some lack of depth and strength.

To many of the students the spirit of American family life was reflected in the interior decorations and arrangement of furniture in the home. They found that colors were gay and cheerful, the arrangement of furniture practical and convenient particularly for room-to-room and in-and-out traffic. They did not, however, find the homes "cozy" and "warm" — there were few if any flowers, very few pictures, and a remarkable absence of reading material save the usual assortment of home and garden magazines, comic books, and sport and news magazines.

About one aspect of American home life, however, there was unanimous agreement. The students were all very agreeably impressed by the mechanical conveniences which they found in almost every home, such as spacious refrigerators, freezers, washing machines, and power lawn mowers. Although many of these are available in Scandinavia as well, the students were impressed by their relatively low cost here, which made such conveniences commonplace even in the homes of the lower-income groups. This latter observation, especially, gave rise to favorable comments.

Art and Culture

The Scandinavian students' observation that there were few books and paintings in American homes did not come as a surprise to them. They had rather expected that "Americans would not be very much interested in cultural matters." This expectation again reflects the visitors' background. There is in Scandinavia a widespread interest in literature, art, and architecture as evidenced in the large number of libraries, the interest and achievement in various forms of textile, glass, and metal handicraft, and in the high standard of Scandinavian design both in buildings and in furniture.

Later on, the students' impressions of American achievements in these arts changed considerably.

I don't think it is correct to say the Americans have no interest in what is often called "culture." I don't know where you would find so many phonographs and even classical records as in American homes. I do think though that they treat the matter differently. Often someone will be very anxious to know the composer's name and the number of a certain symphony when it is playing on the radio or record player, but once they have found out, they seem to find it in good taste to continue talking and laughing instead of listening. I think it is with this as with many other things — they just don't take it so seriously, they don't go into it so deeply.

The students' interpretation of artistic appreciation and accomplishments in the United States altered in another respect. Almost all claimed to have come upon several isolated expressions of outstanding artistic attainment — a building, a piece of sculpture, or an especially well-trained church choir. The impact of such experiences and the generalizations they caused are well exemplified by the remark of one student after a considerable stay in this country:

I still don't think that the aesthetic — and for that matter the intellectual — maturity of the average person here is as high as at home. Of course, you don't have to watch TV very long to see at least one good reason for that! But you find many very fine examples of art and music and architecture. What bothers me is that there is so little pattern or style to it all. Take most any street here in town — the architecture of the buildings is all mixed up. Many buildings are half this and half that, with something entirely different right next to it. And the way the cities are planned and laid out — there is no over-all plan or scheme which can make a city both beautiful and practical to live in. You'll see it in many homes too, particularly the older ones, where the furniture seems to be bought piece by piece with no sense of what it looks like put together. There seems to be a lack of thoroughness in their appreciation of art.

The last two quotations serve well as examples of a fairly uniform pattern characteristic of the way in which the students' impressions of many other aspects of American society changed during their stay. Their relatively vague and undifferentiated preconceptions were being re-evaluated in the light of specific incidents and personal experiences. Out of these emerged an increasingly differentiated picture, the various parts of which were eventually tied together by some underlying themes. Though in individual persons the steps in this process were accompanied by positive, neutral, or negative feelings — depending on the subject matter, the individual's preconceptions, and his personal sojourn experiences — there seemed, in general, to be a corresponding sequence to the students' value judgments. This sequence was characterized by initially positive reactions, followed by a change toward increasingly negative feelings which subsequently turned back in the positive direction.

Recreation

The Scandinavian students were very critical of American commercialized spectator sports which, in contrast to the many individually oriented sports of Scandinavia — such as skiing, hiking, and track sports — provided so little physical exercise for the majority of those attending. Very few of them went to any of the university sport events, but the exuberant, noisy, and almost child-like enthusiasm of the fans on football weekends added importantly to the picture the students were forming of America. Those few who did go to football games soon became avid fans, and some even followed the local team to out-of-state games. The majority were left untouched by the enthusiasm, and it is fair to say that the recreational facilities and opportunities were disappointing to many of them. This was partly a result of their recreational interests. The skiing conditions around the university were poor, and few could afford to travel to better areas. In response to the question "What about your own country have you missed most while here?", practically all mentioned fresh air and natural facilities for individual outdoor recreation.

In keeping with the traditional Scandinavian emphasis on maintaining physical fitness through various forms of bodily exercise, several took daily walks or did workouts in public parks in the early morning hours. Several of these students were stopped and questioned by police on different occasions because they were walking rapidly or running in remote streets. The students' assertion that people in the United States have become so unaccustomed to using their legs that running was subject to attention from policemen was hardly meant seriously, but their impression that deviant behavior was watched closely was further substantiated.

Besides being skeptical about the recreational value of spectator sports, American movies, and television programs, the students were particularly disappointed by the lack of active participation in physical recreation on the part of the average American. Their comments about the "50,000 people sitting down watching 22 individuals carry a ball around" were indeed numerous and unflattering. Although many of these comments were made in jest and good spirit, the students' images of America were undoubtedly influenced by observations of "child-like worship of some few sports heroes" and "excessive reliance on entertainment rather than creative and active forms of recreation."

Although many of the Scandinavian students were unable to carry on their favorite hobbies and spare-time activities as fully as they may have desired, it should not be assumed that they were left disgruntled and with nothing to do in their spare time. Several eventually joined various organizations or clubs which emphasized outdoor recreation. And a number formed a soccer team among themselves and arranged games with other foreign-student teams. In these ways most found some outlet for their recreational interests. However, it must be said that few of them ever developed favorable impressions of American recreational life.

Religious Life

The religious homogeneity of the Scandinavian countries is pronounced. More than ninety-eight per cent of the population belongs to the Lutheran State Church. But the number of people who attend church regularly is fairly small, especially among the younger people. To only a relatively limited extent do churches in Scandinavia serve recreational, welfare, or missionary purposes. Beyond paying a state church tax, few of the people contribute money to the church for such causes. Of the forty students in this study, only two or three were seriously concerned with religious thinking and practices.

These brief generalizations may be helpful in understanding the visiting Scandinavians' remarkable impressions of religion in the United States. In fact, there probably was no aspect of American culture which puzzled the Scandinavian students as much. Having arrived with rather vague ideas and neutral feelings about religious life here, the students' early observations led to the impression of a great deal of diversity and much competitive activity among denominations. In view of the religious homogeneity of Scandinavia, this impression could perhaps have been expected, especially since the students were being energetically catered to during their first weeks here by many student and community religious groups. The students were further amazed by the large number of persons who went to church regularly. Their surprise in this respect could perhaps also have been anticipated, because most of them considered themselves even less religiously inclined than their average fellow countrymen. However, the Scandinavian students soon came to a conclusion about American religious practices which is less readily comprehended: most agreed that the motivation behind church attendance fell short of being genuine.

People here go to church a lot more than they do at home, but I can't help but feel the whole thing is quite dishonest. It seems that you are pressured into joining and participating. Then, also, there is too much concern with money. Why, they collect it in the church — you can even hear it jingle! I've also heard that they come around and have you sign up for a certain amount each year. It somehow reminds you of a business establishment! That time I went to my landlord's church they danced and ate lutefisk in the basement. That was awfully strange. Religion is much more like a kind of recreation here — it's almost like a club. I, personally, consider religion as strictly an individual matter and I don't care to be pushed or to have my beliefs publicized.

Only two or three of the Scandinavian students went to church regularly while here; some went occasionally, but the majority never attended. In the light of this, it is surprising that the students' impressions of religious life in the United States were so firm and consistent. Again, the reason may be sought in the students' religious backgrounds. An outstanding feature of religious thinking in Scandinavia is the belief that true religiosity is incompatible with a concern for worldly goods and money. Religious thinking in many circles in Scandinavia seems further to be characterized by pessimism and the rejection of enjoyable things on the grounds that they are sinful. Only one or two of the Scandinavian students openly shared this conviction — the rest would be more likely to point to this school of thought as a reason for their own religious liberalism; but insofar as they rejected the seeming compatibility of religion and worldliness here, they may be said to have been influenced by this ascetic view. Finally, it should be pointed out that Scandinavian culture imposes a certain restriction on the expression of religious feelings; in fact, people are brought up to be cautious about showing any emotions whatsoever.

The image of American religious life of the majority of students did not change noticeably, although their feelings about it became more neutral. Several came to look favorably on the division of church and state, if for no other reason than the financial advantage of not having to pay church tax. But it is important to note that a decided change occurred in the impressions of those few Scandinavian students who took an active part in church life in America.

There isn't the sharp division between religious and nonreligious people as you find at home. I think that's a healthy thing. I know that American religious life is often called sensational, but it's got to be that way; it's the way of life here. And frankly, I like it that the services here are more colorful; it isn't as dull as at home. I like the choirs they have very much. I also like it that the students are more open about their religion. They also accept more within the church here than we do at home; it isn't so strict.

Economic Life

As a group, the Scandinavian students considered themselves somewhat conservative in comparison with the general population in their home country. Their stay here reinforced their conservatism. They were very favorably impressed by the high standard of living enjoyed by most people in the United States. Specifically, they were overwhelmed by the low prices of automobiles, which made ownership of a car the rule rather than the exception, even for low-income people. Several managed to finance the purchase of a used automobile while here, and it should not be left unmentioned that many of the Scandinavian students spent a large portion of their free time window-shopping and trading equipment and goods of various sorts, including automobiles and optical and electronic equipment. Practical-minded, often with a bent toward technology, the students were struck with the abundance of goods and the relatively unrestricted market in which they could be traded. In fact, several far exceeded the stereotypical American in their preoccupation with gadgets and goods. Herein lies a major reason why the mention of materialism as a characteristic American trait declined in frequency during their visit — the meaning of the concept began to change.

I think Americans are materialistic, but actually that is all right with me. After all, I'm beginning to think that I'm that way myself. I like to make money too! And I particularly like the way things are done efficiently here. For example, before I came here I had never given a thought to this matter of time and motion in industry. I've really gotten my eyes opened to — well, all these things — efficiency, economy, salesmanship, advertisement, or business in general, you might say. I like that very much and I'm frankly quite disgusted with my own country in these respects. They restrict economic life so much that you can't apply these principles. Even though my field of study isn't business, I'll say that I have been influenced most during my stay here by what you might call the commercial or business people in the United States.

The reasons the Scandinavian students advanced for the high standard of living in the United States fell into two categories. Some emphasized rich natural resources as the most important source of its wealth, and often were critical of the manner in which the fruits of these resources were distributed. The natural wealth was seen, too, as a basic reason for the development of certain American traits. Excessive spending and installment-plan buying (which they felt, incidentally, raised the standard of living artificially, giving a false impression) and the lack of concern for property used by the public, such as railroad stations, movie theaters, and sidewalks — all these were thought by some to reflect the carefree, self-confident, aggressive, even reckless and inconsiderate nature of many Americans. To other students, the basic reason for the booming American economy was to be found in the free-enterprise system which stimulated the intensive and daring effort of a few to utilize the vast resources this country had been endowed with and rewarded them for their ingenuity and foresight.

In the eyes of this latter group of students, this system had contributed much to the development of the typically industrious, practical-minded, self-confident, enthusiastic, aggressive, and efficient American business personality. Although important changes took place during their stay, the students' views on the merits and disadvantages of the free-enterprise economic system were usually closely related to their liberal-conservative orientation back home. But whatever their economic orientation, they all strongly disapproved of having their own countries labeled socialistic in the derogatory sense in which the term was used by some Americans.

Political Life

The Scandinavian students all considered themselves and their countries as belonging to the Western political faction. Before coming here, their interest in American politics had been largely confined to issues of foreign policy, particularly those which in some way affected their own countries. They knew little about American domestic political problems. This emphasis was maintained during their visit as well. Unless their own countries' prestige or welfare was involved, the Scandinavian students were altogether uninterested in American political thinking and practices. They rarely took part in the discussions or attended the lectures on political issues offered by the various campus organizations. As a result, their images of American political life were influenced mainly by contemporary events. The 1952 presidential campaign, which took place while many were in this country, was often cited as illustrative of the low standards of politics in the United States. This impression was augmented by their observations of the various measures taken to guard internal security.

I don't think Americans think independently about politics. It's quite frightening how slogans and persons rather than ideas dominate. They can be swayed to vote for a candidate on the basis of how cute his grandchildren are. Then, their entire approach to this communist issue seems kind of ridiculous; America is losing her freedom because of it; it's very tragic. What really annoys me is that they don't seem to see the difference between the social democracies of Scandinavia and the totalitarian socialist dictatorship of Russia. They ask you how it feels to be in a free country! Apparently they aren't very well informed. Also, they often talk about the waste in sending aid to other countries, when, in effect, it is very beneficial to themselves as well. Certainly I can't see that they can have anything to complain about as far as the way the Marshall aid was used in Scandinavia.

The question of postwar American aid to the Scandinavian countries was of particular concern to the students. This was one of the few instances in which their national prestige was involved and they felt in a strong position to deny the contention by some Americans that economic aid to foreign lands is not appreciated and often not put to good use.

The Scandinavian students' ideas about American political thinking and behavior fit a familiar pattern: superficial attention to issues of public concern, exemplified by reading of headlines rather than serious study; lack of independent thought and action as evidenced by the naive means of persuasion used in political campaigns and by rapidly changing public opinion and sentiment; and unpremeditated generosity in aiding others, followed by impatience if the aid is thought to be ineffectively applied.

Social Stratification

In respect to social stratification in America, the students' preconceptions were again very limited. Actually, most of their prearrival impressions about this aspect were based on observations of the relations between officers and privates among American troops stationed in Europe: as compared with the German army, the social structure of the American army was much less rigid. Beyond these observations, their preconceptions were confined to some general ideas about the United States as a country where the possibilities for economic success were great, and where wealth rather than family background determined a person's social position.

With the exception of brief visits to Chicago or New York, the students' impressions of social stratification in the United States were based mainly on observations in the Madison area. Those who secured part-time jobs while here were very much pleased by the lack of social consciousness in employer-employee relations. They found this informal atmosphere pleasant personally and saw in it great advantages in work incentive and output. During an informal discussion of this topic, one student pointed out that this free relationship between boss and workers in America was carried to the point where it endangered the discipline necessary in the management of a large business; however, his comment was quickly countered by two other students, both with job experience, who assured him that "this informality from above goes only so far." In spite of these differences of opinion, these students as well as many others expressed a strong desire for more friendly, equalitarian, and informal employer-employee relationship in Scandinavian industries and institutions.

The picture of social stratification in the United States which the Scandinavian students eventually developed was one which showed a definite hierarchy of socioeconomic classes, in which the emphasis placed on social factors is minimal in comparison with the importance attached to economic gain, with the consequence that social relations among the classes are not greatly affected. About the only negative reaction was the revulsion that some students felt for the slums they had seen in some of the larger cities.

Race Relations

Before coming, the Scandinavian students thought of American racial problems as almost exclusively a Negro-white problem and almost entirely confined to the South. Their prearrival attitudes toward our treatment of Negroes were overwhelmingly unfavorable. During their stay here their images of racial and ethnic relations changed considerably, if not in feeling at least in content.

The same friendly informality and apparent equality which the Scandinavian students had observed in people's social, recreational, and occupational activities generally and in parent-child, student-professor, and employer-employee relations specifically also characterized their early impressions of relations between the races. Whatever opportunity this community gave them to observe interaction between Negroes and whites left them with the impression that at least in everyday personal relations there are few if any signs of discrimination.

Later on, the students began to voice their surprise about finding evidence of prejudice against Jews. For a limited number of the Scandinavian students, their reaction to living in a racially and ethnically mixed society took the form of rather pronounced prejudices against minority groups. But it should be emphasized that the number of students who were observed to develop prejudices against minority groups was small indeed. The majority did not react in this way, and most Scandinavian students felt that they had arrived at a much more complete understanding of the complexity of race relation problems in the United States as a result of their visit here.

Personality

Perhaps the most striking single feature in the Scandinavian students' impressions of American personality, deriving from their association with fellow students and their interaction with other Americans in a wide variety of casual and institutional settings, was the lack of any pattern of personality or character traits which they associated with Americans as a nation.

The two characteristics that the Scandinavian students mentioned most frequently in describing their relations with Americans were "friendly informality" and "conformity." Although they often interpreted the friendly informality of Americans as superficial, as time passed many of the students came to have a high regard for this trait and expressed the wish that social relations at home, particularly among students and teachers and employers and employees, might have more of this quality. The strain of Americans toward conformity, especially in political and economic thinking but also in dress, recreation, and religion, was often commented on. This trait was not highly valued and many of the Scandinavian students found it particularly inconsistent in a society with a long and proud tradition of individualism. Even in these characteristics wide variations were perceived among Americans, and it would be erroneous to infer that the Scandinavian students thought of them in any real sense as national character traits.

A number of other characteristics were perceived and freely discussed. Americans were described as carefree, active, happy-go-lucky, kind, fresh, flippant, friendly, noisy, exuberant, immature, generous, superficial, informal, optimistic, enthusiastic, ebullient, aggressive, self-confident, hard-working, sociable, practical, inconsiderate, and efficient. There was no contradiction in this description; rather, these adjectives indicate the wide range of the students' views and were expressed in particular situations at different times and with different value judgments intended. For example, the fresh informality, the ebullience, and the aggressive drive of the American businessman were admired by many as important in the commercial and technical advances of the United States. However, the same general kind of behavior often evoked quite different and sometimes opposite reactions when it was carried over into social situations. Thus, American businessmen were viewed as superficial, flippant, noisy, and rude in many of their nonbusiness relations. American students were frequently regarded as immature, superficial, and uninterested in intellectual matters, but at the same time were considered friendly, generous, kind, self-confident, and practical. Many other illustrations could be given of specific characterizations of this sort but they would all point to the same tendency of the students to perceive American personality selectively and differentially.

Trends in Impressions

Up to this point, the Scandinavian students' impressions of American life have been presented in terms of specific areas of content. Not only the nature of these impressions but also the change in attitudes has been stressed. Now a more adequate idea of the trends in the students' impressions can be got by comparing their responses in the early interviews with those in later sessions. To facilitate this comparison, we made a crude quantitative summary of the interview materials dealing with each student's first impressions, subsequent impressions, and final (predeparture) impressions of some fifteen areas of American life. This was done by rating the student's responses for each area on a five-point scale ranging from "very favorable" to "very unfavorable." These ratings were then summarized to give a general measure of the degree of favorableness of each student's impressions of American life, and the summary scores were categorized as "favorable" or "unfavorable."

The distribution of these summary scores at the three different times (see Table 3) indicates that (a) a large majority of the students had good first impressions of the United States; (b) after several weeks had passed, the impressions of American life held by a slight majority of the visitors were generally unfavorable; (c) the students' impressions became generally favorable again before they left.

Table 3. Distribution of Students by Summary Score on Attitudes toward the United States at Three Different Times

Attitude	First Impressions	Subsequent Impressions	Final Impressions
Unfavorable	10	21	14
Favorable	30	19	26
Total	40	40	40

Taken at face value, Table 3 shows that the number of students with unfavorable impressions of American life just before departure was greater than the number at the first interview. This requires some explanation. In a large degree this apparent decrease in affect is the result of the fact that many students had unrealistic first impressions based on their favorable preconceptions and the enthusiastic welcome they received during the early days of their sojourn. These impressions soon became less favorable as the demands of academic work and the adjustment to day-to-day living made life less glamorous. In fact, a counter-reaction set in and some of the students became disillusioned, tended to withdraw, and grew bitter about life in America. As time passed, most of them adjusted to the realities of the situation and came once more to view American life favorably — although much more realistically than before. Now, most of them evaluated the host society more equivocally than at first. Their impressions, whether favorable or unfavorable, were usually qualified and tended to vary according to the aspect of the culture under consideration. Of course, there were a few students who, because of frustrating experiences here, became more unfavorable toward American life as time passed; but for the most part those whose final impressions were unfavorable were the ones whose first impressions were unfavorable — suggesting that factors in their own background and personality may have been important determinants of their attitudes.

It is not, however, the comparison between the students' first impressions and final impressions which is particularly interesting, but rather the U-shaped developmental trend of their impressions. This finding, which emerged clearly from the interview material and from observation of the students' behavior, was further substantiated by the results of the students' self-ratings. During the last interview they were asked to depict the trend in their impressions on a graph with two axes — time periods during the sojourn and general feeling toward the United States. In almost every instance, the students drew U-shaped curves, suggesting that they perceived their own impressions as being very favorable during the early days and weeks of their stay, becoming less favorable for a time, and then turning increasingly favorable as the end of the sojourn approached.

The explanations which the students gave of the shape of the curves they had drawn are interesting not only because they reveal the students' awareness of their own difficulties in adjusting to the new culture but also because they call attention to some of the reasons for this typical pattern.

There is a dip here shortly after I arrived because I was mad at everything. Everything was different and you had to study all the time — but it was probably my own fault, not because of the Americans. Now it [the curve] has gone up a lot because I understand things more.

In the very beginning I was very happy because everything was new and exciting. Later, here, the curve drops because the novelty wore off. Now it's back up here because I'm getting used to things and getting into it more.

Before I came I thought very well of America. After all, they helped to liberate my country. Then after I had been over here a while the curve dropped. Now it has gone back up again some, but, it's a funny thing, when I'm with Americans I argue for Norway, but when I'm with Norwegians I defend the United States.

After I came, it [the curve] was very low. It was perhaps mostly because of this credit transfer trouble. Things were really unpleasant. Now it has increased, and I think it will go up more after I return home because I'll forget the little things that made me mad.

From all of the evidence it appears that the Scandinavian student's sojourn was characterized by an adjustment cycle in which there was first a brief period of relatively favorable impressions of the United States, which was then followed by a period of less favorable feelings, and finally by a period characterized by increasingly favorable views.[1] The highs reached by students' impressions and the lows to which they dropped varied considerably from student to student, but the general pattern was the same for virtually every member of the group.

Conclusions

The one most striking similarity among the Scandinavian visitors was the selectivity with which they perceived major aspects of American life and the objectivity with which they evaluated these perceptions. As a matter of fact, only a few students tended to react globally and emotionally to the foreign environment. Although they were not at all uncritical in their appraisal of the American culture, the Scandinavian students' views and judgments of different aspects of American life were often completely independent of their impressions of other areas. Only with limited clarity did themes in the visitors' perceptions emerge that embraced several different content areas. There was some tendency, for example, to view American family life, art, architecture, religion, and politics as superficial. Another theme in the students' impressions centered on their observation of Americans as less individualistic or more conforming than expected in social, moral, religious, and political behavior. But no clear-cut idea of American personality emerges from the students' reactions.

Finally, significant changes in the Scandinavian students' impressions of the United States occurred during their stay. These changes were found to follow a developmental trend characterized by initial relatively favorable impressions of the United States followed by a period of less positive feelings which, in time, again grew more favorable. Thus, the students were at first favorably impressed with America and left with favorable impressions but for a period during the stay found much that they did not like about American life.

CHAPTER

5

———

Relationships of Selected Variables to Outcomes

ONE of the important aims of research in cross-cultural education is to isolate important characteristics of the individual student as well as significant features in his sojourn experience which contribute to the attainment of the goals attempted in foreign educational programs. Expressed purposes of international exchange programs have tended to emphasize large aims which, because of their generality, are difficult to assess. Moreover, many of them are not particularly pertinent to student visitors. Accordingly, it becomes necessary to postulate a set of plausible goals which have specific relevance for university students and about which information is obtainable. A number of such reasonable outcomes may be outlined.

Obviously, one of the first would be that the visiting students make adequate adjustments to the academic environment as reflected in their academic achievement during the sojourn and in the attainment of their educational purposes. A second objective would be maximum participation in the life of the host country. This goal is based on the assumption that association with the people and institutions of the host society will result in better understanding and appreciation of that culture and perhaps of other cultures as well. A third goal is that the visiting students develop favorable impressions of the host country, or at least that their impressions become more favorable during their stay. In turn, one may foresee that such favorable attitudes may result in the visitors' desire to adopt selected features of the host culture both during the sojourn and after they return home. Underlying these aims is

55

the expectation on the part of everyone concerned with student exchange that, whatever their specific purposes in coming, the visitors will be satisfied with the foreign experience in general.

The Variables

Once this tentative and somewhat limited set of goals is accepted, an important aim in an exploratory study of this nature is to isolate some of the variables in the students' background, intellectual orientation, personality, and academic and social situation which are related to these outcomes. To implement this aim six outcome variables reflecting the achievement of the goals already mentioned were arbitrarily selected for detailed analysis. These outcome variables are participation in American life; academic adjustment at the university; final impressions of the United States; change in impressions of the United States; attitude toward adoption of selected American features; and satisfaction with the sojourn.

Other outcome variables were available from the data of the study, but we felt that these six were the most important, and that they would at least serve as a representative selection. On the basis of information from the interviews and other sources, the students were rated not only on the six outcome variables but also on twenty-seven others. In all, then, each student was rated with respect to thirty-three variables dealing with a wide variety of aspects of his background, personal orientation, personality, academic and social situation, and outcomes of the sojourn. A list of these variables classified according to the above categories is given in Table 4. (A description of the variables, along with a more detailed explanation of the basis of the ratings, is given in Appendix 5.)

The relation between each of the six outcome variables and all other variables was determined and expressed in correlation coefficients.[1] Those with a magnitude of .30 or greater are listed and discussed under the headings of each of the selected outcome variables below.[2] All of the coefficients are presented in Table 5.

Participation in American Life

Advocates of international student exchange generally agree that active participation in the life of the host culture is an important means to gaining a realistic picture and a sympathetic understanding of its

Table 4. Classification of the Selected Variables, Direction, and Number of Categories

Classification of Variable	Direction	No. of Categories
Background		
Age	Young to old	8
Residential background	Rural to urban	8
Socioeconomic status	Low to high	10
Leadership in home country	Low to high	9
Academic performance in secondary school	Low to high	10
Previous contacts with other cultures	Low to high	10
Previous contacts with U.S.	Low to high	10
Prearrival impressions of U. S.	Unfavorable to favorable	8
English-language facility	Low to high	9
Mental ability	Low to high	8
Personal orientation		
Political orientation	Liberal to conservative	10
Intellectual orientation	Practical to theoretical	10
Nationalism	Low to high	9
Definiteness of career plans	Indefinite to definite	9
Purpose of sojourn	Socio-cultural to professional-technical	10
Freedom from preoccupation with home culture	Low to high	8
Personality		
Social ease	Low to high	10
Personal flexibility	Low to high	10
Freedom from defensiveness of self	Low to high	10
Dependency	Low to high	8
Personal adjustment	Low to high	7
Academic and social situation		
Guidance	Low to high	9
Academic prestige loss	Low to high	8
Financial support	Low to high	10
Freedom from frustrations	Low to high	9
Arrival impressions	Unfavorable to favorable	10
Length of sojourn	Short to long	10
Outcome		
Participation	Low to high	10
Academic adjustment	Poor to good	7
Final impressions	Unfavorable to favorable	10
Change in impressions	Less to more favorable	10
Transfer of U.S. features	Less to more	10
Satisfaction with sojourn	Low to high	8

major features. Through observation, travel and study, the visiting Scandinavians all learned much about the United States, but differences in motivation and opportunity resulted in considerable variation in the extent to which they developed personal contact with Americans and actively took part in the daily life and special events of the host community.

The ratings on participation in American life were based on the following specific information: proportion of spare time spent in social activities carried on in the company of Americans; extent of contact with the American community, i.e., churches, industries and businesses,

Table 5. Correlation of Selected Variables with Outcome Variables

Variables	Participation	Academic Adjustment	Final Impressions	Change in Impressions	Transfer of U.S. Features	Satisfaction with Sojourn
Background						
Age	−.49	−.05	−.32	−.23	−.40	−.14
Residential background	.47	−.02	.23	.05	.14	.14
Socioeconomic status	.37	.18	.30	.13	.16	.31
Leadership in home country	.29	.33	.13	.07	.18	.26
Academic performance in secondary school	.15	.09	−.08	.07	.03	.07
Previous contacts with other cultures	.52	.26	.27	.27	.14	.29
Previous contacts with U.S.	.71	.44	.37	.30	.21	.40
Prearrival impressions of U.S.	.39	.04	.38	.27	.45	.02
English-language facility	.79	.34	.31	.23	.12	.31
Mental ability	.18	.34	−.17	−.15	−.25	.30
Personal orientation						
Political orientation	.05	.14	−.10	.04	−.14	.07
Intellectual orientation	.21	.30	.10	.20	.06	.29
Nationalism	−.43	−.28	−.33	−.30	−.26	−.33
Definiteness of career plans	.52	.02	.30	.30	.35	.07
Purpose of sojourn	.58	.39	.58	.66	.48	.47
Freedom from preoccupation with home culture	.78	.32	.55	.50	.53	.42
Personality						
Social ease	.42	.16	.27	.26	.33	.14
Personal flexibility	.71	.68	.64	.51	.28	.60
Freedom from defensiveness of self	.28	.51	.35	.06	−.08	.46
Dependency	.34	.23	.61	.52	.41	.27
Personal adjustment	.25	.68	.28	.05	−.15	.61
Academic and social situation						
Guidance	.73	.50	.59	.51	.44	.44
Academic prestige loss	−.46	−.48	−.63	−.43	−.36	−.65
Financial support	.43	.19	.26	.15	.19	.30
Freedom from frustrations	.36	.74	.63	.35	.16	.70
Arrival impressions	.24	.51	.68	.51	.33	.55
Length of sojourn	.23	−.17	−.16	−.16	−.02	−.18
Outcome						
Participation		.36	.56	.38	.41	.34
Academic adjustment	.36		.57	.39	.12	.73
Final impressions	.56	.57		.76	.62	.55
Change in impressions	.38	.39	.76		.64	.46
Transfer of U.S. features	.41	.12	.62	.64		.15
Satisfaction with sojourn	.34	.73	.55	.46	.15	

families, and commercial recreation activities; extent of dating with Americans; and participation in campus organizations and events. The significant relations found indicate that *the greater the student's participation in American life*

Correlation Coefficient

BACKGROUND VARIABLE

—the better his English-language facility.................... .79
—the greater his previous contacts with U.S. culture........ .71
—the greater his previous contacts with other cultures...... .52
—the younger his age..................................... .49
—the more urban his background.......................... .47
—the more favorable his prearrival impressions of the U.S.... .39
—the higher his socioeconomic status...................... .37

PERSONAL ORIENTATION VARIABLE

—the less he was preoccupied with the home culture......... .78
—the more socio-cultural his sojourn purposes.............. .58
—the less definite his career plans........................ .52
—the less his feelings of nationalism...................... .43

PERSONALITY VARIABLE

—the greater his personal flexibility...................... .71
—the greater his social ease.............................. .42
—the greater his dependency.............................. .34

ACADEMIC AND SOCIAL SITUATION VARIABLE

—the more guidance he received........................... .73
—the less he suffered academic prestige loss................ .46
—the better his financial support......................... .43
—the more favorable his first impressions of the U.S......... .56
—the less he suffered frustration......................... .36

OUTCOME VARIABLE

—the more favorable his attitude toward transfer of U.S.
  traits .... .41
—the more favorable the change in his impressions of the U.S. .38
—the better his academic adjustment...................... .36
—the greater his satisfaction with the sojourn.............. .34

It is not necessary to comment in detail on these findings. Apparently most of the variables in each of the categories are related to participation in American life. The background characteristics seem to be of particular importance, as indicated by the number of variables in this category which correlate modestly to highly with participation. The five variables with highest coefficients are English language facility (Background), previous contacts with the United States (Background), freedom from preoccupation with the home culture (Personal orientation), personal flexibility (Personality), and the amount of guidance received (Academic and social situation). In general, it is readily apparent that each of these facilitates the visiting student's communication with Americans. The only relationship which perhaps requires explanation is that between guidance and participation. The guidance variable is an index of advice and direction on academic and personal matters received from several sources, such as fellow students, roommates, and teachers, as well as the foreign student adviser. Judging from the interview material and observation of the visitors' behavior, they appeared to benefit markedly from such guidance in increased social ease and confidence. The data also suggest that advice and guidance, especially on personal matters and social behavior, was more available to those students who, through active participation, established relatively close friendships with Americans. Considering that the Scandinavian students came from a society the norms and behavior patterns of which are in many respects very similar to those of the United States, this finding suggests that foreign students from cultures which differ greatly from the American may need considerable advice and counsel if they are to take part extensively in American life.

The long list of correlations between participation and other variables can be simply summarized as follows: students who are young and from high status urban backgrounds, who have good English-language facility, who have had extensive prior contacts with the United States and other countries, whose sojourn purposes are not narrowly defined and specifically professional, who are personally flexible and at ease in social situations but who seek and use guidance when needed, and who encounter few frustrations in academic and social affairs are the ones who tend to participate most fully in American life. Moreover, a high level of participation is associated with favorable attitudes toward the United States as indicated by favorable final impressions of American life and culture, more positive affect over time, and desire to see selected American culture traits adopted in the home country. Good academic adjustment and general satisfaction with the sojourn are associated, also, with participation in American life.

Academic Adjustment

Of all the goals of foreign study the one most important to the student is the educational experience itself. For the student, the success or failure of his foreign visit hinges in large part upon his ability to adapt satisfactorily to the new educational situation. This does not mean that he must completely accept the academic norms of the host university in order to get passing grades; some of the Scandinavian students made good marks despite their rejection of some of the norms (see Chapter 3). But it does imply that for the greatest educational gain from his visit he must make a satisfactory adjustment to the new academic situation. The Scandinavian students were given ratings on academic adjustment based on interview responses, teachers' ratings, and advisers' comments. Data from these sources were combined to form an index designed to measure the students' willingness and ability to accept the norms of the University and to perform their academic responsibilities in a manner which would be acceptable to them and their teachers.

The correlations of academic adjustment with other variables reveal that *the better the student's academic adjustment at the University*

*Correlation
Coefficient*

BACKGROUND VARIABLE

—the greater his prior contacts with the U.S. 44
—the better his English-language facility .34
—the higher his mental ability 34
—the greater was his leadership at home .33

PERSONAL ORIENTATION VARIABLE

—the more socio-cultural his sojourn purposes 39
—the less he was preoccupied with the home culture 32
—the more theoretical his intellectual orientation 30

PERSONALITY VARIABLE

—the better his personal adjustment 68
—the greater his personal flexibility 68
—the less his self-defensiveness 51

ACADEMIC AND SOCIAL SITUATION VARIABLE

—the less he suffered frustration 74
—the more favorable his arrival impressions of the U.S. 51
—the more guidance he received 50
—the less he suffered academic prestige loss 48

OUTCOME VARIABLE

—the greater his satisfaction with the sojourn................ .73
—the more favorable his final impressions of the U.S......... .57
—the more favorable the change in his impressions of the U.S. .39
—the greater his participation in American life.............. .36

From these coefficients it is apparent that background characteristics and personal orientation variables, which were of considerable importance in explaining participation in American life, are relatively less important than personality and academic and social situational variables in relation to academic adjustment. Such factors as English language facility, previous contact with the United States, and lack of preoccupation with home culture, although they still play a part, appear to be less basic than are good personal adjustment, freedom from defensiveness of self, personal flexibility, freedom from frustrations, lack of academic prestige loss, and favorable arrival impressions. Though there may be spurious elements in some of these correlations, because of the difficulty in making independent ratings of academic adjustment and various aspects of social adjustment, there is considerable supporting evidence from interviews and observations that personality and social situation variables played a major part in the long-term academic adjustment as well as the day-to-day academic adjustment of this group of students.

If the relatively modest correlations found between academic adjustment and other variables are kept in mind, the following tentative conclusion is justified: Students with good English language facility, who had extensive previous contact with the United States, whose prearrival and first impressions of the United States were favorable, who were leaders in their own country, who had high mental ability, whose orientation was primarily intellectual, whose sojourn purposes were not narrowly defined, who had little preoccupation with the home culture, whose personality adjustment indicated personal flexibility, freedom from defensiveness of self, and freedom from frustrations, who sought and used guidance when needed, and who did not suffer academic prestige loss tended to make a good academic adjustment. Good academic adjustment was also associated with the other outcome variables, but was most clearly related to satisfaction with the sojourn and final impressions of the United States. This demonstrates the important influence that academic experiences have in determining other important outcomes of foreign study, at least for this group of students.

Final Impressions of the United States

One of the most frequently sought and expressed goals of cross-cultural education programs is that the visiting students will, as a result of their sojourn, become favorably disposed toward the country visited. The hope and expectation is that their attitudes will be favorably influenced as they take part in and come to understand more fully the host society's way of life. This outcome may be measured either by ascertaining the degree of favorable affect at the close of the sojourn or by measuring the trend in impressions over time. Both are important and both are used in this analysis. The former will be considered here. A presentation of the variables associated with change in impressions will follow the discussion of final impressions.

The ratings of the students' final impressions of the United States are based on their responses to questions designed to elicit their attitudes toward some fifteen aspects of American life and culture such as family life, government, the economy, religion, education, art, social relations, race relations, architecture, personality, philosophy, and technology. Each student received a score on each aspect. These scores were summed to obtain a total score, the results were cast into an array, and the array was divided into categories indicating the degree of favorableness to American life and culture. The resulting measure was then correlated with each of the other thirty-two selected variables. The significant correlations indicate that *the more favorable the student's final impressions of the United States*

Correlation
Coefficient

BACKGROUND VARIABLE

—the more favorable his prearrival attitudes toward the U.S.. .38
—the greater his prior contacts with the U.S................ .37
—the younger his age....................................... .32
—the better his English-language facility.................. .31
—the higher his socioeconomic status...................... .30

PERSONAL ORIENTATION VARIABLE

—the more socio-cultural his sojourn purposes.............. .58
—the less he was preoccupied with the home culture........ .55

—the less his feelings of nationalism...................... .33
—the less definite his career plans......................... .30

PERSONALITY VARIABLE
—the greater his personal flexibility....................... .64
—the greater his dependency............................... .61
—the less his self-defensiveness........................... .35

ACADEMIC AND SOCIAL SITUATION VARIABLE
—the more favorable his arrival impressions of the U.S....... .68
—the less frustration he suffered........................... .63
—the less he suffered academic prestige loss................ .63
—the more guidance he received............................ .59

OUTCOME VARIABLE
—the more favorable the change in his impressions of the U.S.. .76
—the more favorable his attitude toward transfer of U.S.
  traits .... .62
—the better his academic adjustment....................... .57
—the greater his participation in American life.............. .56
—the greater his satisfaction with the sojourn............... .55

The highest correlations with the student's final impressions of the United States are with academic and social situation variables and personality variables. Although several of the background variables meet the arbitrary level set, none seems to be of great importance. Personal flexibility, willingness to seek guidance, freedom from frustration and from academic prestige loss, and favorable arrival impressions appear to be among the most important factors in determining favorable final impressions of the United States.

However, taking into account all of the correlations, the indications are that those students with greatest contact with this and other cultures, who are young, from high status families, whose English is good, who do not have strong emotional ties to the home culture, who have social and cultural sojourn purposes with indefinite career plans, who seek advice and counsel from others, who are personally flexible and not defensive, and who suffer few frustrations and little academic prestige loss are more likely to leave with the most favorable impressions of the United States. Moreover, the students whose final attitudes toward America are most favorable tend to be the ones whose attitudes have become more favorable during the sojourn, who have made good academic adjustments, who have participated widely in American life, who are well satisfied with the sojourn experiences, and who have favorable attitudes toward the adoption of selected American culture traits by their home countries.

Change in Impressions of the United States

This outcome variable differs from the previous one in that it attempts to measure change in the attitudes of the students during the course of their sojourn. It was derived from the responses of the students to questions about aspects of American life and culture asked during the first and last interviews, approximately nine months apart. The responses during the first interview were scored in the same manner as those in the final interview, and the ratings represent the degrees of difference or change over time.

The correlations of this variable with the other selected variables indicate that *the more favorable the change in the student's impressions of the United States*

Correlation Coefficient

BACKGROUND VARIABLE

—the greater his prior contacts with U.S. culture.............. .30

PERSONAL ORIENTATION VARIABLE

—the more socio-cultural the purposes of his sojourn......... .66
—the less his preoccupation with the home culture.......... .50
—the less his feelings of nationalism...................... .30
—the less definite his career plans....................... .30

PERSONALITY VARIABLE

—the greater his dependency............................ .52
—the greater his personal flexibility..................... .51

ACADEMIC AND SOCIAL SITUATION VARIABLE

—the more guidance he received......................... .51
—the more favorable his arrival impressions of the U.S....... .51
—the less he suffered academic prestige loss................ .43
—the less frustration he suffered........................ .35

OUTCOME VARIABLE

—the more favorable his final impressions of the U.S......... .76
—the more favorable his attitude toward transfer of U.S.
  traits .... .64
—the greater his satisfaction with the sojourn.............. .46

—the better his academic adjustment...................... .39
—the greater his participation in American life............. .38

Actually, this set of correlations differs little in content from those of the variable *final impressions of the United States*. The only difference is that the correlations with change in impressions are generally lower and, as a consequence, some dropped below the arbitrary level set for this study. This was particularly true of the background variables. None of the variables which fell below the required standard on the final impressions measure increased in magnitude in relation to the change in impressions measure. Consequently, the interpretations made with respect to final impressions hold, except to a lesser degree, and no further explanations of the correlations need to be given.

Attitude toward Adoption of Selected American Culture Traits

One goal of international student exchange that many people would count as important is that the visiting students develop a favorable attitude toward the selective adoption of aspects of the host culture by the home country. This is certainly important when the visitors come from a technologically less advanced country to study in a country that is more advanced. And it is of importance even when the levels of technical development of the two cultures are not greatly different because it helps to facilitate communication and avert misunderstandings between the two countries. In a sense, willingness to adopt characteristics from the host culture represents a test of the scope and genuineness of the visitors' favorable attitudes. To get data on this variable, each student was asked during the last interview, "What features, if any, of American life would you like to see transferred back to your own country?" Some mentioned very few or no characteristics that they thought worth adopting; others mentioned several, from specific technological improvements to economic policies. On the basis of number, type, and scope of the suggestions, the students were divided into categories of greater or less willingness to consider the transfer of selected features of American culture to their home countries. The ratings on this variable were then correlated with each of the selected variables. The significant correlations indicate that *the more favorable the student's attitude toward the adoption of selected American traits by the home country*

Correlation
Coefficient

BACKGROUND VARIABLE

—the more favorable his prearrival impressions of the U.S..... .45
—the younger his age................................... .40

PERSONAL ORIENTATION VARIABLE

—the less he was preoccupied with the home culture......... .53
—the more socio-cultural the purposes of his sojourn......... .48
—the less definite his career plans......................... .35

PERSONALITY VARIABLE

—the greater his dependency.............................. .41
—the greater his social ease.............................. .33

ACADEMIC AND SOCIAL SITUATION VARIABLE

—the more guidance he received........................... .44
—the less he suffered academic prestige loss................. .36
—the more favorable his arrival impressions of the U.S....... .33

OUTCOME VARIABLE

—the more favorable the change in his impressions of the U.S.. .64
—the more favorable his final impressions of the U.S.......... .62
—the more his participation in American life................ .41

It is apparent that of the six outcome variables, the students' attitude toward adoption of American traits correlates least with the other selected variables. None of the relationships is very high nor is there any very noticeable concentration in any particular category. One reason for this may well be that the saliency of this particular goal of foreign study is not nearly so great for Scandinavian students as it would be for students from countries whose technological and political development is less advanced than that of the United States. The students did not talk much about this question, which resulted in difficulties in differentiating among them. Differentiation on this dimension was limited in the other direction by the fact that none of the visitors rejected transfer of American features in any universal or violent fashion. Their recommendations were generally reasonable and specific and they were sufficiently confident of their own countries' achievements and standards that there was no cause for emotional defensiveness.[3]

With these qualifications in mind the following tentative generalization can be made: those students who are younger, whose impressions of the United States were consistently favorable, who were not particularly preoccupied with the home culture, whose career plans and sojourn purposes were not narrowly defined, who tended to be somewhat dependent and to seek and use guidance, who were at ease in social situations, and who suffered little academic prestige loss tended to have favorable attitudes toward the adoption of selected American culture traits at home. Those with higher ratings on this variable were more likely to have participated widely in American life and to have more favorable final impressions of America but were not noticeably more satisfied with their sojourn nor did they make markedly better academic adjustments than did those whose ratings were lower.

Satisfaction with the Sojourn

Probably there would be no advocate of student exchange programs who would not agree that as a minimum result of the sojourn the visitors should go home feeling satisfied with their foreign experiences. Only one of the Scandinavian students left the United States feeling greatly disappointed. A few said that some of their hopes and aspirations for the sojourn fell short of being fully realized, but most were well satisfied with their visit. This information came from each student during a portion of the final interview devoted to discovering the extent to which the students' various sojourn purposes had been accomplished and, in addition, the degree to which they were satisfied with the foreign experience. From their responses it was possible to assign each student to one of several categories of degree of satisfaction with the sojourn experiences. The resulting rating was then correlated with the other selected variables. The correlations indicate that *the greater the student's satisfaction with the sojourn*

*Correlation
Coefficient*

BACKGROUND VARIABLE

—the greater his prior contacts with the U.S....................... .40
—the higher his socioeconomic status......................... .31
—the better his English-language facility.................... .31
—the higher his mental ability............................. .30

PERSONAL ORIENTATION VARIABLE

—the more socio-cultural his sojourn purposes............... .47
—the less his preoccupation with the home culture........... .42
—the less his feelings of nationalism....................... .33

PERSONALITY VARIABLE
—the better his personal adjustment...................... .61
—the greater his personal flexibility...................... .60
—the less his self-defensiveness........................... .46

ACADEMIC AND SOCIAL SITUATION VARIABLE
—the less he suffered frustration.......................... .70
—the less he suffered academic prestige loss................ .65
—the more favorable his arrival impressions of the U.S....... .55
—the more guidance he received........................... .44
—the greater his financial support........................ .30

OUTCOME VARIABLE
—the better his academic adjustment at the university....... .73
—the more favorable his arrival impressions of the U.S....... .55
—the more favorable the change in his impressions of the U.S.. .46
—the greater his participation in American life.............. .34

From these correlations it is apparent that a number of variables dealing with the student's background, personal orientation, personality characteristics and with the academic and social situation have bearing on his satisfaction with the sojourn. Again, the personality and academic and social situation variables seem to be most important. It is quite understandable that those students whose personality adjustments are good will tend to find satisfaction with the sojourn experiences. The central emphasis placed by this group of students on the importance of academic aspects of the sojourn is clearly reflected in the correlations between academic and social situation variables and satisfaction with the sojourn. Again, the interrelationship between this variable and the other outcome variables is notable, particularly its high relationship with academic adjustment and the variables dealing with impressions of the United States.

In summary, it appears from these coefficients that there is a tendency for students with good English language facility, high socioeconomic status, high mental ability, extensive prior contact with the United States, favorable arrival attitudes, weak psychological ties with the home country, social and cultural sojourn purposes, good personal adjustments, and favorable academic and social experiences at the University to be most satisfied with their sojourn experiences. Satisfaction with the sojourn is also highly related to good academic adjustment, favorable impressions of the United States, and participation in American life.

Variables Most Consistently Associated with Foreign Study Goals

The results of this analysis of the relationship among selected outcomes of foreign study experiences and selected variables in students' background, personal orientation, personality, and academic and social situation have indicated the importance and potential fruitfulness of further research into the correlates of the achievement of goals in programs of this kind. This analysis has shown the pattern of relations among each outcome variable and all the other variables. These patterns have been summarized throughout the chapter and need not be repeated here. However, it may be profitable to comment briefly on the variables which have been found to be related consistently to the outcome variables.

It is apparent that several *background variables* as defined in this research are significantly associated with half or more of the desired outcomes. The correlations suggest a tendency for young students who have high English-language facility, extensive prior contacts with the United States, favorable prearrival impressions, and high socioeconomic status to participate extensively in American life, to have favorable impressions of the United States, to make good academic adjustments, to favor the transfer of selected American culture traits to the home culture, and to be well satisfied with their sojourn in the United States. Of these, the prior contact measure and the rating on English-language facility are the two most commonly and highly associated with the outcome variables. Apparently even in a group which generally has very good command of English, facility in speaking English is of considerable importance if students are to take part in and accept the host country's life and culture, to make good academic and social adjustments, and to enjoy the sojourn. Earlier contacts with the United States also seem to have a very important bearing on the attainment of these goals of foreign study. Scandinavian students have many opportunities for contact with American life and culture through American visitors to Scandinavia, American relatives, books, magazines, and movies. Those who utilize these opportunities most fully come to the United States with greater knowledge and willingness to adjust to American norms, feel freer to participate in social life, find academic and social adjustment relatively easy, maintain their favorable attitudes, and are satisfied with the foreign experience.

The fact that the younger, high status students and those with favorable preconceptions make the best adjustments squares well with expectations. The younger students from higher status levels probably are relatively less committed to jobs and dependents in their own countries and are more likely to seek the stimulation of a new society and to be able to afford the time and money to participate in it to a greater extent than the older students from lower status backgrounds. Of course, it might well be expected that favorable preconceptions would stimulate the students to take part more fully, to make good adjustments, to be likely to continue to view American life favorably, and to enjoy the sojourn.

Although the analysis has indicated some interesting and important relationships between the background and outcome variables, it is notable that several of the background measures which were expected to have an important bearing on outcomes of the sojourn did not. For example, prior contact with other countries, intelligence, and such aspects of experience in the home country as residential background, leadership, and academic record in secondary school bore little relation to the outcomes as measured in this study. It is possible that the crude measures we employed masked real relationships between these and the outcome variables. It is probable that the restricted variation among the students on some of these variables lowered the correlations. In any event, the results should not be taken to mean that these factors are unimportant in selecting students for foreign study. At most they show, for this group of students, that once the students have been selected, individual differences on these measures are not particularly associated with projected goals of foreign study. It is possible that other background variables not measured would show a greater relationship to the outcome variables.

Four of the five *personal orientation variables* employed in this analysis are associated significantly with most of the desired outcome variables. The measures of preoccupation with the home culture and purposes of the sojourn are significantly related to each of the outcome variables, and the measures of nationalism and definiteness of career plans are significantly related to four of the six outcome variables. The directions of these relationships suggest that students who are relatively free from strong psychological ties to the home country as evidenced by lack of preoccupation with the home country and relatively little feeling of nationalism, who have indefinite career plans, and whose sojourn purposes are more social and cultural than technical or professional are the ones who are likely to gain the most favorable impressions of the United States, to make the best academic adjustments, to favor the transfer of selected American culture traits to the home country, and to be most satisfied with their visit. It should be pointed out that the measures employed for rating political and intellectual orientation bore little relationship to any of the outcome variables.

Three of the five measures of *personality variables* were highly related to half or more of the outcome variables. Personal flexibility, dependency, and freedom from defensiveness of self were all clearly associated with the desired outcomes. It is not surprising that students with more personal flexibility and freedom from defensiveness of self should find it possible to take part fully in another society, would tend to be more sympathetic with its ways, and would make good academic and social adjustments. But the reason why greater dependency is associated with favorable outcomes of the sojourn is perhaps not so obvious. A possible explanation of the relationship is that a certain amount of willingness to seek the help of others is necessary if the students are to take part extensively in the life of another society and to make successful adjustments to its academic and social norms. It can be hypothesized further that the resulting participation and adjustment are likely to promote favorable attitudes and a feeling of satisfaction with the sojourn experiences. On the other hand, the explanation may be that those students who are most dependent on the help of others are prone to be less critical in their evaluation of the host society and culture. At least it would appear that some willingness to depend on others is a prerequisite for the attainment of many of the goals of foreign study. The two remaining personality variables — social ease and personal adjustment — were each closely related to two of the outcome variables. The relations found between this limited set of personality measures and the outcome variables indicates the potential fruitfulness of further study of personality variables in future studies of cross-cultural education. A wider coverage and better measurement of personality variables than was possible in this study may be very rewarding, especially for research on selection of students and prediction of the outcomes of foreign study.

Four of the six *academic and social situation variables* were consistently related to the outcome variables. Two had moderate to high correlations with all six outcome measures. These were the measures of the amount of academic prestige loss the student thought he had suffered and the amount of guidance he had received during the sojourn. In general, the less the student had suffered academic prestige loss and the more guidance he had received, the more favorable were his scores on the outcome variables. If a student thinks his past academic achievement is underestimated by the host university, this apparently influences negatively not only his academic adjustment but also his participation and attitudes toward the host society and his satisfaction with the sojourn. The extent of guidance sought and received appears to be a fairly powerful influence on participation in American life, academic adjustment, final impressions of the United States, and satisfaction with the stay. Despite the fact that the Scandinavian students were mature and able persons who needed relatively little guidance in order to get along here, the advice and coaching they received appeared to be related to the outcome of their sojourn in several important respects. It is probable, too, that the relation between the frustration measure and the outcome variables was influenced by the fact that those receiving the most guidance had the fewest frustrating experiences. These findings are all consistent with informal observations that the students who achieved the favorable outcomes were carefully guarded from frustrating experiences here and were carefully guided throughout their stay.

Finally, the arrival impressions of the students seemed to have a lasting influence especially on the outcome variables dealing with subsequent attitudes toward the adoption of selected American culture traits. The two situational variables that bore little relation to outcomes of the sojourn were financial support during the sojourn and the length of the sojourn. This does not mean that financial support and length of sojourns are unimportant in the achievement of goals in foreign study programs. Actually, financial support, even though it was not a great problem for this group, was consistently associated with the outcome variables although in only two instances were the coefficients .30 or greater. Length of sojourn might have been of more importance had there been a greater range in the length of stay. On the average, the students were here for sixteen months and none was here for less than nine months.

It may be concluded from this limited analysis that aspects of the academic and social situations may have considerable influence on the outcomes of foreign study. In future studies more emphasis might well be placed on these and other matters in the social and academic situation in which foreign students must function. In particular it seems advisable to examine as many aspects of the academic situation as possible with a view to finding ways of making academic adjustment easier for foreign students, since much of the evidence of this study suggests that whatever the sponsoring agencies may have in mind, the foreign students themselves are concerned mostly with reaching their academic goals. Especially, it seems to me, the importance to successful student exchange of such factors as the extent of prestige loss and the extent and type of orientation and guidance appears to warrant further investigation by specialists.

One of the most striking results of the correlation analysis attempted in this study is the consistent interrelationship among the *outcome variables*. Of the fifteen possible interrelations, thirteen are high enough to meet the standards used in this study. Participation, final impressions, and change in impressions all have moderate to moderately high correlations with all other outcome variables. Academic adjustment and satisfaction with the sojourn are both related to all outcome variables, except adoption of selected culture traits. The direction of the relationships is in all cases positive, indicating that a favorable outcome in one area is associated with favorable outcomes in the other areas. This finding, if confirmed by other studies, seems to suggest that there is a process or mechanism at work which promotes success in general in cross-cultural education. At least the results of this study suggest that participation in American life leads to favorable impressions of the United States and that the more favorable the impressions, the more one participates; good academic adjustment not only stimulates participation but also is in some measure the result of participation, and both, in turn, result in more favorable impressions of America and a greater willingness to see American culture traits adopted in the home country. Finally, all of these reciprocal influences are reflected in a high level of satisfaction with the sojourn experiences. Whether or not this finding has more general applicability and whether or not other outcomes not included in this analysis would also be found to be interrelated with this cluster of variables, is a matter for further research. But the tentative results presented here indicate that much might be gained by giving considerable emphasis in future studies to the interrelationship among the goals of foreign study programs.

Conclusions and Implications

THE general purpose of the study was to explore the academic and social adjustment processes and outcomes of foreign study. This was done by focusing intensively on forty students from Scandinavia who were attending the University of Wisconsin during 1952–54. The specific objectives of the study were (1) to get information about the academic and social adjustments of the students; (2) to get information about the content and feeling tones of the visiting students' impressions of the United States as well as the changes in these impressions during the sojourn; (3) to examine the relationship between factors in the students' background, intellectual and sociopolitical orientation, personality, and sojourn situation, which together and separately might have bearing on the students' academic and social adjustment, satisfaction with the sojourn, and images and impressions of the United States; (4) to discover possible promising leads and hypotheses for further research; and (5) on the basis of these findings, to make tentative suggestions for the guidance of student exchange.

The data came mostly from guided interviews with the students throughout the course of the sojourn. These were supplemented by information acquired through participant observation, teachers' and advisers' ratings, and university records.

This information was processed in such a way that both descriptive and quantitative analyses were possible, depending on the objectives.

The exploratory nature of the study requires that the findings should be considered as suggestions for a relatively new field of scientific inquiry rather than as established facts.

Academic Adjustment

The Scandinavian students came to a university which has a tradition of treating American and foreign students alike. As do many American students, the visitors found registration somewhat confusing and some felt that the university did not justly evaluate their past academic records and accomplishments. This feeling was most common among students who seemed less well adjusted personally and it was often associated with subsequent unfavorable impressions of various aspects of the American university system, especially academic standards and supervision of students. Other aspects of academic life that were commented on unfavorably were the relatively rigid routine of the university — compulsory class attendance, day-to-day assignments and frequent objective examinations, and the regulation of students' activities and social life. But the Scandinavian students were very favorably impressed by the informality of relations between students and teachers and the quality of many aspects of instruction. As time passed, they accommodated to the local academic norms, although many of them never came to accept them.

The academic adjustment problems the Scandinavian students encountered did not, however, prevent them from being highly successful in their academic work as indicated by the high grade point averages, the high ratings and favorable evaluations given them by their teachers and advisers, and by their own evaluations of their accomplishments. The undergraduate Scandinavian students earned a slightly better grade point average than did the entire undergraduate student population at the university, and the visiting Scandinavian graduate students did exceptionally well.

This record was reflected in the teachers' ratings and advisers' opinions of the visiting students on various criteria pertaining to academic adjustment and performance, classroom conduct, and ability. These ratings and opinions were generally high. In the eyes of their professors, the Scandinavian students were responsible and mature persons of excellent mental ability. They adjusted easily to the academic environment and made rapid academic improvement.

Social Experiences and Adjustment

Socially, the Scandinavian students appeared to adjust with ease to campus and community life at this American university. Their reasons for participating in social activities varied greatly. Likewise, there were considerable differences among them in respect to various traits facilitating easy social interaction with strangers. As a consequence, the nature and extent of the Scandinavian students' participation in American life differed greatly and the manner in which they adjusted socially varied from one person to the next. Despite these individual differences, a limited number of clearly defined social behavior types could be detected into which most of the students could be fitted: *detached observers, promoters* of home country features, *enthusiastic participants* in American life, and *settlers.*

Generally, the Scandinavian students were very well satisfied with their social experiences in the United States. The large majority of them stated that they could think of no changes in their experiences which would have resulted in more adequate fulfillment of their desires in this respect. The rest of the students were less satisfied only because they felt they had not had time and opportunities enough to associate with Americans.

Impressions of American Life

Information about the Scandinavian students' perceptions of American culture and changes in their attitudes was obtained through questioning in content areas including American family and home life, recreation, religion, race relations, and economic and political life. The results showed not only that the students' perceptions and reactions varied considerably but that as a group they were highly selective and objective in their views and appraisal of these various features of American life. Only a few students tended to react in an undifferentiating and emotional fashion. Nevertheless, their impressions of each of these aspects showed sufficient similarities to form distinguishable patterns which could justly be used to describe the group of visitors as a whole.

Careful examination of the interview protocols revealed further that besides these patterns a few themes appeared around which aspects of the students' impressions in various content areas tended to cluster. For example, a considerable number of the adjectives used by the students in describing American norms centered on the concept of superficiality. This theme reached into their perceptions of American moral and religious behavior, art appreciation, and political thinking and behavior, but it applied particularly to social relations. This perception was not always accompanied by negative feelings. Many of the students, for example, saw much virtue in the light, informal, and noncommittal kind of social interaction found to be typical of America. In fact, the features of American life which the students were most desirous of transferring back to their own cultures concerned human relations — both at the everyday social level and also in respect to professor-student and employer-employee relations. A second group of the adjectives employed in the students' description of American culture centered on conformity. In their eyes, independent contemplation and genuine conviction were often lacking in American moral, religious, and political thinking and behavior. The students found that the pioneer spirit of rugged individualism and respect for originality which had figured importantly in their preconceptions of America had yielded to a mass culture where conformity was of prime importance.

By rating the students' responses to the questions about the various aspects of American life covered in the series of interviews according to degree of favorableness, quantitative data about attitudes were obtained. A comparison of the ratings in early interviews with those in later ones revealed that changes in the Scandinavian students' attitudes toward the United States took a sharply defined developmental trend. This trend was characterized by relatively favorable initial impressions of America, followed by a period of less positive attitudes which turned in time into more favorable ones. The Scandinavian visitors arrived here with generally favorable views of this country and they left with impressions which were also primarily favorable.

Relationships among Selected Variables

The Scandinavian students were rated on a large number of variables concerning background, personality, and personal orientation characteristics as well as various factors related to the sojourn situation and experiences. The ratings were based largely on systematic coding of interview responses. From these variables, thirty-three were selected for further analysis. Six of the selected variables — participation in American life, academic adjustment, final impressions of the United States, change in impressions, satisfaction with the sojourn, and attitude toward adoption of American features in the home culture — were treated as outcome variables because they represented characteristics commonly considered desired goals or effects of foreign-student exchange.

The relationships between the outcome variables and the twenty-seven other variables were analyzed and as a result, patterns of relationships were discovered between the various independent variables and each of the outcome variables. In addition, it was found that selected independent variables were consistently related to all or most of the desired outcomes. Students with such favorable background characteristics as high English language facility, extensive prior contact with American culture, and high socioeconomic status were found to have favorable attitudes toward American life, to make favorable academic adjustments, to enjoy their sojourn, and to favor the transfer of selected American culture traits to the home culture. Likewise, such personal and intellectual orientations as lack of preoccupation with the home culture, freedom from nationalistic feelings, social and cultural sojourn purposes, and indefiniteness about career plans were consistently and closely related to favorable outcomes of the sojourn. Personality variables — particularly personal flexibility, dependency, and freedom from self-defensiveness — were commonly associated with achievement of the desired goals of foreign student exchange. The two situational variables most highly and consistently related to sojourn outcomes were the amount of formal and informal guidance the student had received and the extent to which he felt that he had suffered prestige loss. In general, the less the student had suffered loss of prestige and the more he had received guidance, the better was the outcome of the sojourn as measured in this study. Finally, a relatively high and consistent interrelationship among the outcome variables themselves was found, suggesting that attainment of goals of foreign study in one area is linked with attainment of goals in other areas or activities.

Some Practical Implications

The present investigation was not specifically designed as an evaluation of the practices and procedures of sponsoring agencies and university personnel concerned with foreign students. Nor was it planned specifically to evaluate the outcomes of a foreign study program. Rather, it was an exploration into the nature of the processes involved in foreign students' learning and adjustment. Nevertheless, during the course of the research and especially by virtue of the intensive interviews, findings emerged which we believe have practical implications for administrators and others concerned with foreign students' welfare.[1] They will be summarized in this section. It is important that these findings be considered as suggestive rather than final and particularly that caution be taken in generalizing them to other groups of foreign students in other kinds of academic and social setting. However, the determination of foci of research in this area will no doubt continue to be influenced significantly by the need for solution to problems of a practical nature in international student exchange and by the insight and recommendations of foreign-student advisers and others who have close continuous contact with foreign students. The observations presented here may therefore well be directed to these people for evaluation in light of their own experiences.

One of the difficulties encountered by some of the Scandinavian students in this study resulted from the plurality of their sojourn purposes. Many of them had been granted scholarships designed primarily for attainment of sociopolitical goals. As recipients of these scholarships, they tried to some extent to play the role of culture carriers or ambassadors of good will by learning informally as much as possible about American institutions and by seeking contacts with American people. But by reason of their own desire or in their role as students at the university, subject to its requirements, these visitors also felt obliged to spend much of their time and efforts on their academic work while here. As a result, some of them felt that their sojourn purposes had not been fully realized because they had been torn among several objectives. No doubt the typical American campus provides an ideal setting for the establishment of cross-cultural contacts between foreign students and Americans from many walks of life. It is possible, however, that the two kinds of purpose of foreign-student exchange — academic and sociopolitical — may best be accomplished if a clearer distinction is made between them, and their attainment sought through different types of programs.

Although most of the Scandinavian students eventually made satisfactory adjustments to the university, many of their initial adjustment difficulties might have been avoided if they had been better informed before arrival about various details of the American university system. Especially the translation of past academic records into so-called credits proved to be troublesome to many and a source of great concern to some. It is very likely that if more information about entrance requirements, credits, grades, semester hours, required courses, class attendance, quizzes, tests, papers, assignments, and general supervision of students were available abroad, the prospective visiting students would then be in a better position to comprehend the more specific information pertaining to the policies and practices of individual American universities usually included in the bulletins available from such schools upon request.

The problems of transferring academic credits from one institution of higher learning to another are not confined to cross-national transfers. However, in international student exchange these problems are particularly difficult, primarily because the basis for evaluation and formal assessment of students' success varies greatly from one country to another and among universities in the same country.

The matter of transfer of academic records seemed to be of considerable importance to the adjustment and success of these foreign students. This points to a need for further objective evaluation of the relative standards of secondary and higher education in different countries throughout the world. The Institute of International Education, the American Association of Collegiate Registrars and Admissions Officers, and the National Association of Foreign Student Advisers are all concerned with this problem and are making efforts to cope with it. But it will no doubt be many years before adequate appraisals will be available for all countries. Meanwhile, it would be well if prospective foreign students were encouraged to bring with them to the new university some of the most important textbooks and outlines of courses which they have covered in their major field of study. These would be useful to departmental advisers at the American university in determining the level of placement and courses to be taken.

Throughout the presentation of the findings of this study we have referred to the U-shaped developmental trend in the Scandinavian students' reaction and adjustment. If this pattern applies to foreign students of other nationalities, it has certain implications for administrators as well as lay groups concerned with foreign-student exchange.[2] It may be consoling to these individuals to know that the criticisms and generally negative reactions which characterize the intermediate phase of the students' adjustment process are likely to have little bearing upon the final adjustment outcome. As such, it is important that this phase is recognized as a "natural" and perhaps necessary step toward subsequent sojourn success rather than as a failure to adjust. For example, if the tendency of foreign students to withdraw socially, during a certain period, to their own subcultures were recognized as a natural self-defensive maneuver, then the efforts of well-meaning persons and civic groups to provide opportunities for contacts between foreign students and the American community might be continued throughout the sojourn rather than concentrated in the first few weeks or days. Also the advisers and teachers of the foreign students might take cognizance of this trend in adjustment and provide more help and guidance when it is most needed.

Another implication of this finding, if other studies confirm the results of this aspect of the present study, is that those concerned with student exchange as a means of promoting international understanding should give serious attention to the length of the sojourn necessary to achieve the most desired results. The present study furnishes no definite guidance on this point because only students who planned to remain on the campus for a year or more were included. But if the developmental trend in adjustment and attitudes toward the host culture found in this study applies generally, it is obvious that foreign study programs should provide for a long enough sojourn to permit the students to complete the cycle before returning home. Possibly in those cross-cultural education programs whose purpose is to give politicians, labor leaders, farmers, or businessmen a favorable view of a given country, there would be much to recommend short, well-planned, and event-filled visits.[3] In student exchange programs, on the other hand, there is much to be said for visits that will be long enough to give the students an adequate knowledge and appreciation of the country visited rather than uncritical acceptance and unrealistic notions of its ways. Finally, the study offers some evidence that a few students became so closely identified with the host culture that they may have a difficult readjustment to make when they return to their home country — if, indeed, they return at all.

The results of the correlation analysis likewise gave rise to a number of suggestions which may have practical implications. For example, it appeared from this analysis that success in the attainment of sojourn objectives depended to some extent upon the age and general level of maturity of the students. Thus, the younger students who were less committed to careers and dependents at home were very successful in the pursuit of broader sociocultural goals, while the older and more mature students who were already firmly established in careers at home were particularly successful in reaching goals of academic and professional advancement. If this finding holds for other groups of foreign students, it may have practical implications for people concerned with selecting candidates for international student exchange. In the same vein, the students' English language facility warrants attention. This variable was found in this study to be strongly related to several important sojourn outcomes. The same was true for a number of personality characteristics such as personal flexibility and lack of self-defensiveness. Differences in norms and levels of living characterize the setting in which international student exchange takes place. Adequate means of communication and willingness to submit temporarily to different standards seem to be key attributes in successful cross-cultural learning.

Finally, there was much evidence that the Scandinavian students' reactions to this country were heavily influenced by their perceptions of how they, themselves, and their own countries were being perceived and evaluated by Americans. One example of this was seen in their keen interest in the university's appraisal of their academic background, but the awareness was present whether they were being evaluated as students, as sportsmen, as friends, or as Scandinavians. It is likely that the inconsistency in values and norms which often characterizes the psychological situation of the foreign student tends to heighten his self-awareness and to intensify his perception of himself as a member of a specific culture, thus making him especially sensitive to others' appraisals of him.[4] In any event, observation of the group of Scandinavian students suggests that Americans who are interested in their welfare, whether as landlords, fellow students, coworkers, or teachers, should try not to offend foreign students by asking questions and making comments which not only reveal their own ignorance of the visitors' culture but which may also be perceived as a threat to their national status.

Suggestions for Further Research

One of the purposes of this study was to discover leads for further research.[5] A number of problems meriting further study have been mentioned throughout this report. These need not be repeated in detail here. But several challenging substantive and methodological problems which have emerged from the analysis and which need further testing will be mentioned briefly. A number of suggestions for further research which have grown out of the project but to which the present research had relatively less to contribute directly will also be mentioned.

In many ways the most interesting finding of this study was that there is a developmental cycle which appears to be the same for several aspects of students' adjustment to the sojourn situation. Academic adjustment, social adjustment, and attitudes toward American life all seem to follow a cycle, the first phase of which is characterized by favorable adjustment and attitudes, followed later by a considerably less favorable trend, and finally by a phase in which adjustment and attitudes become more favorable again. Some practical implications of this cycle for cross-cultural education have been suggested; however, before more definite theoretical or practical inferences can be drawn, it will be necessary to determine whether or not this cycle is descriptive of the experiences of other groups of foreign students at Wisconsin and on other campuses. If it proves to be, there would be much reason for further research attempting to chart the trend more precisely and to determine what factors in the sojourn experience contribute most to its developmental course.

Another finding of the study on which further research is needed was that a number of factors in the individual's background, intellectual orientation, personality, and in the social and academic aspects of his sojourn are closely and consistently related to the outcomes of foreign study. Some of the practical implications of this have already been discussed; but this finding also suggests various promising research leads. The evidence from the limited correlation analysis made in this study suggests that there may be underlying patterns or constellations of variables which may be of special significance to the achievement of the goals of foreign study programs. Appropriate statistical techniques for identifying these factors might be applied to these and similar data. One experience indicates that careful attention will need to be given to the selection and measurement of variables as well as to sampling problems in such analysis, but we have defined at least some of the variables which should be included.

There is also some reason to believe, on the basis of the correlation analysis, that instruments for prediction of the achievement of certain goals of foreign study might be developed. Before such research could proceed far, however, it would be necessary to have clear statements of the goals of student exchange programs and to develop adequate measures of these and other variables. Some of the variables defined and used in this study should be considered for any prediction instrument of this kind, but there would be need for much ingenuity in developing better indicators of these and other variables.

Another finding of this study which needs to be examined more closely in future research is the consistent interrelationship among the outcome variables themselves. From the relatively crude analysis carried out in this research it appears that success in one area is commonly associated with the achievement of a variety of other goals of foreign study. This suggests some reciprocal relationship between goals, but the data of this study are not adequate to test this hypothesis — much less describe the complex processes that may be at work. We suggest that future studies should be designed to get more information about the nature and extent of this relationship.

In general, the present research was handicapped by our not having adequate data for studying in closer detail the processes at work which produced given effects during the sojourn. The design of the study called for periodic interviews of all of the students, and these were held; but still so much happened to the students between interviews that much of the detail of the adjustment process was missed. Possibly more frequent interviewing or more participant observation than was possible in this study might help to overcome this difficulty. In any event, further research is needed on the processes at work in attitude formation and attitude change, social adjustment, and academic adjustment in cross-cultural education programs.

In the original plan for the study an analysis was contemplated which would stress changes in perceptions, attitudes, and adjustment problems in a sequence of time periods beginning with the students' decisions to come to the United States and ending at the time when they were about to return home. This scheme was handicapped by the fact that some subjects could not recall and put these matters into a time perspective with accuracy. This more detailed plan was therefore abandoned and emphasis was put only on preconceptions, arrival perceptions, and prereturn perceptions and attitudes, but even the limited recall that this necessitated was difficult for many of the students. As a consequence, the data on changes in perceptions and attitudes may be rather blurred. Experience suggests that analysis of change over time is crucial to both the theoretical and the practical aspects of cross-cultural education and that the data on which such analyses are to be based should be obtained at or near the time the experiences occur rather than reconstructed on the basis of recall. In future studies attention should be given to this methodological point.

Another observation is that many of the important effects of the American experience probably cannot be determined while the students are still on the campus. In all probability there are delayed effects on career patterns, subsequent attitudes, and behavior which will be apparent only after the students resume their usual roles at home.[6] There is some evidence from the comments of the Scandinavian students that they think their attitudes may change considerably after they return home and have an opportunity to see their experiences in wider perspective. This suggests that in future research, plans should be made for some periodic follow-up after the visiting students have returned home, to provide a more adequate picture of the effects of sojourn experiences.

Finally, one area of importance which was omitted almost completely in this study has to do with the influence of the visiting students on the members of the host society. From unsystematic and informal observation of the interaction patterns of the Scandinavian students, it was apparent that at least some of the visitors may have had more influence on their fellow students than their American associates had on them. Though this was probably not generally true, there is good reason to believe that the presence of foreign students on an American campus has direct and indirect effects on the attitudes of the local students. In some instances meeting foreign students may produce greater interest and knowledge of international affairs among American students, while in other cases the opposite effect may result. Much more thought and research should be devoted to the reciprocal aspects of foreign study to learn more about the influence of foreign students on the attitudes and behavior of Americans.

APPENDIXES, NOTES, BIBLIOGRAPHY
AND INDEX

APPENDIX 1. INTERVIEW GUIDE

I. ARRIVAL EXPERIENCES AND IMPRESSIONS

A. *Arrival in the U.S.*
  1. When did you arrive in the U.S.?
  2. Where did you land?
  3. Did anybody *meet you?*
  4. What were your impressions of *custom* and *immigration* procedures?
  5. *How long* did you stay in New York?
  6. *What did you do* during your stay in New York? (sightseeing, eating, nightclubs).
  7. Did you go around *alone or with somebody?* (finding places, getting around).
  8. What about *people*, in the streets, stores, bars or restaurants did you notice?
  9. Do you recall any particularly *pleasant* experiences or impressions from your first days in America?
  10. Was there anything about America (Americans) that *disappointed* you or surprised you unpleasantly?
  11. What were your *over-all impressions* of America at that point?

B. *Trip to Madison*
  1. *How* did you get to Madison?
  2. Did you *talk with anybody* on the train (bus, plane)?
  3. What did you see or hear on the way that you recall as being *unexpected* or surprising?

C. *Arrival in Madison — Registration*
  1. Did anybody *meet you* when you came to Madison?
  2. Did you know where you were going to *live?* How did you find a place?
  3. *What did you do* before school started? In the daytime, at night? Did you go around *alone* or with somebody?
  4. Could you tell me about *registration* and getting enrolled?
  5. Did anybody *advise* or *help* you? Did you get an adviser? Was he helpful?
  6. Were you satisfied with the *recognition you got for your work back home?*
  7. How did you decide on the *courses* to take?
  8. What was your *over-all impression* of registration and the University?

9. What were your impressions of the way you were *received and taken care of?*

10. What are some of your impressions of the way your *sponsoring agency* has handled your case? (financial, advice, efficiency, giving you freedom of choice and action) .

D. *Early School Orientation*

1. What did * you think of the way *classes* were conducted? (methods of teaching, teacher-student relationship).

2. What did you think of *attendance, exams, and assignments?*

3. How did your *fellow students* impress you? (scholastically, socially).

4. What are your *over-all* impressions of education in America at this point?

E. *Early Social Experiences*

1. With whom did you *spend most of your spare time* during those first weeks?

2. How did you spend your *spare time* — evenings and weekends?

3. Did you join any *organizations* and *clubs?*

4. Did you feel that you were *accepted by others* as well as any other student was? As well as any other foreign student?

5. When people learned that you were from Scandinavia what were some of the things they were interested in finding out about? What kind of questions did they ask?

6. What do Americans expect a *Scandinavian* student to be like?

7. How did you feel about the prestige your nationality gave you? How did it compare with the prestige of other nationalities in the eyes of Americans?

8. How did you feel about the sincerity of Americans' interest in you as a foreign student and in your country?

9. Did you try in the beginning to contact your *countrymen* in order to be with them?

10. What percentage of your spare time have you spent with fellow Scandinavians as compared with Americans?

11. What do you usually talk about with fellow Scandinavians here?

F. *First Impressions by Content Area*

1. Aesthetic matters (art, architecture, music, literature, houses, cities, parks, interior decorating, furniture, designing).

2. Economic matters (economic stratification, standard of living, commercialization, free enterprise).

3. Family life (husband-wife relationship, wife's role, upbringing of children, marriage, divorce, old people).

4. Crime, law, and social control (law obedience, police, justice, equality).

* Depending on how long the student has been at the university at the time of this interview, the questions will be phrased in the present or the past tense.

5. Minority groups (Negroes, Jewish people, ethnic groups, race riots, slums).
6. Politics (*domestic*: interest in political affairs, caliber of politicians, social security, patriotism, meaning of freedom, democracy, the press; *foreign*: aid, NATO, tariffs, United Nations, Russia).
7. Recreation (sports, competition, spare time activities, hobbies, interests, radio, movies, TV, drinking).
8. Religion (church-going, diversity, importance in daily life, sincerity).
9. Sex-social behavior (dating, rules governing young people's behavior, attitude toward sex, moral standards).
10. Social relations (friendliness, number of friends, depth of friendships, social codes).
11. Social structure (social classes, class consciousness, employer-employee relations).
12. Technology (material comfort, standard of living, technical devices, gadgets).
13. Values and philosophy of life (what are Americans interested in? what do they want to get out of life? what is an "ideal" life to Americans? materialism, optimism, rights, freedom, individualism, aggressiveness).

II. BACKGROUND INFORMATION

A. *Residence*
  1. Where were you born?
  2. How long did you live there?
  3. What was your house like?
  4. What kind of people lived around there?
B. *Education*
  1. Where did you go to elementary school?
  2. Which subjects did you like best? Least?
  3. How did you get along with the other kids?
  4. How did you compare with the other pupils educationally?
  5. Where did you go to high school?
  6. What line of study did you follow?
  7. Which subjects did you like best? Least?
  8. How did you get along with the other students? Teachers? How did you like school?
  9. How did you compare with your fellow students academically?
  10. Did you continue in the university?
  11. How well did you do there?
  12. What degrees did you hold before you came to the U.S.?
  13. Could you tell me about the traveling you did before you came to America?

C. *Occupation*
1. What do you plan to do for a living?
2. Is this your own choice?
3. What kinds of jobs have you had in the past?
4. Were there any changes in your occupational goals? Why?

D. *Family*
1. How many brothers and sisters do you have?
2. What does your father do for a living?
3. How does his income compare with that of other people in your country?
4. What would you say your parents' social standing is compared to others in the community?
5. How did your family get along together?
6. Which person in your family are you most like? Which do you feel closest to? What is he (she) like?

E. *Social Relationships and Role*
1. What kind of hobbies and interests have you had in the past?
2. Would you say you made friends easily?
3. Did you have a wide circle of friends compared to others your age?
4. What kinds of organizations and clubs did you belong to? Did you hold any offices?
5. How would you describe a couple of your closest friends?
6. How do you think they would describe you to someone else?
7. What do you think your friends liked most about you? Respected you most for?
8. Are there any things that some people didn't like about you?
9. What would a person be like that you would dislike very much?

F. *Reference Groups and Dependency*
1. If you had a serious personal problem, something which required the help of someone else, whom would you talk it over with?
2. What group of people in your country would you say came closest to having the same ideas as you had with regard to politics, economics, religions, national affairs?
3. Compared to others, how much would you say you depended on other people? Whom? With regard to what?

III. PRECONCEPTIONS

A. *Plans for U.S. Stay*
1. When did you first decide to come to America?
2. Why did you want to come to the U.S.? What did you expect to gain from it?
3. How or why did you choose the University of Wisconsin?
4. How much did you know about the work you would be doing?
5. How long did you expect to stay?

6. Did you plan on getting a degree?
7. Did the wishes or desires of anyone else play an important part in your planning?
8. How did you plan to get financial support? Did this affect your plans as to how long you would stay?
9. What plans did you have for housing?
10. Which places did you plan or expect to visit in America?
11. Did you consider any plans for naturalization?

B. *Academic Preconceptions*
1. What were some of your ideas about what going to school here would be like?
2. What did you expect with regard to the difficulty of university work here as compared to home?
3. What were your preconceptions about teaching methods? Exams? Grades? Attendance? Assignments? Caliber of teachers and students?
4. What did you expect campus life to be like?

C. *Status and Role Preconceptions*
1. With the educational background you had, where in the university system did you expect to fit in?
2. What sort of prestige did you think your nationality would have in the U.S. compared to other nationalities?
3. What sort of ideas did you think Americans would have about Scandinavia(ns)?
4. How did you think prestige was determined in American schools? In America generally?

D. *Sources and Nature of Preconceptions*
1. From which sources did you get most of your ideas and information about the U.S.?
2. What ideas and information did you get from school, books, movies, magazines, radio, newspapers, relatives (letters or visit), American tourists, soldiers, returned Scandinavian students?
3. Could you tell me about Americans you met before coming here?
4. How would you have described an American before you came here?
5. Did you expect Americans to be more like other nationals or more like your own?
6. What about Americans did you particularly like or dislike?

E. *Preconceptions by Content Area*
1. Aesthetic matters (art, architecture, music, literature, houses, cities, parks, interior decorating, furniture, designing).
2. Economic matters (economic stratification, standard of living, commercialization, free enterprise).
3. Family life (husband-wife relationship, wife's role, upbringing of children, marriage, divorce, old people).

4. Crime, law, and social control (law obedience, police, justice, equality).
5. Minority groups (Negroes, Jewish people, ethnic groups, race riots, slums).
6. Politics (*domestic*: interest in political affairs, caliber of politicians, social security, patriotism, meaning of freedom, democracy, the press; *foreign*: aid, NATO, tariffs, United Nations, Russia).
7. Recreation (sports, competition, spare time activities, hobbies, interests, radio, movies, TV, drinking).
8. Religion (church-going, diversity, importance in daily life, sincerity).
9. Sex-social behavior (dating, rules governing young people's behavior, attitude toward sex, moral standards).
10. Social relations (friendliness, number of friends, depth of friendships, social codes).
11. Social structure (social classes, class consciousness, employer-employee relations).
12. Technology (material comfort, standard of living, technical devices, gadgets).
13. Values and philosophy of life (what are Americans interested in? what do they want to get out of life? what is an "ideal" life to Americans? materialism, optimism, rights, freedom, individualism, aggressiveness).

F. *Realism of Preconceptions*
1. Considering what you know now, which of these areas did you find most like the way you expected it to be? Which ones were most different?
2. In general, what do you consider the most important shortcomings about your preconceptions?
3. In what areas is it most important for a student to know what he is going into? Why?
4. What could be done (by themselves or others) to give students who come here a more realistic picture of conditions in America?

IV. EXPERIENCE IN RESIDENCE

A. *Contacts with Home Culture*
1. What sort of things in your home country have you missed the most while here?
2. What percentage of your spare time here have you spent with fellow Scandinavians? What did you usually do?
3. How much time do you spend with fellow Scandinavians now compared with the first 1 to 2 months here?
4. How much have you spoken Norwegian (Swedish, Danish) compared with English while here?

5. How often have you read your country's newspapers (magazines, books)?
6. How much have you been in contact with people of Scandinavian descent (U.S. relatives, Sons of Norway, Ydun Lodge, Ygdrasil Society)?
7. How often have you gone to the Scandinavian Club meetings?
8. Have you been a member of the International Club? How often have you attended meetings?

B. *Social Interaction with Americans*
1. Which clubs and organizations have you belonged to?
2. Who are the Americans you have had most contact with while here? Fellow students, fellows on your job, people in the community, organizations and clubs, recreation, dating?
3. How much of your spare time do you spend with Americans now as compared with the first 1 to 2 months here?
4. Has the fact that you are a foreign student influenced the extent to which you have been accepted by Americans and invited to take part in social activities? In which direction?
5. Do you think this is true for foreign students in general, from all countries?
6. If you were to start all over again on your stay in America would you try to make any changes in your social activities? Are you satisfied?
7. Do you think that your stay here will influence your social prestige once you return to your own country?
8. How much traveling and touring have you done? Any traveling plans?
9. What or who do you feel have influenced you the most during your stay here in your outlook on America? Who or what have you learned most from?
10. Which group of people in America (educationally, professionally, intellectually, politically, economically, socially) do you feel closest to? Which group comes closest to agreeing with your outlook on life?
11. Have your own views changed while you have been here with regard to political, economic, or religious matters? Have you become more liberal or more conservative?

C. *Subsequent Impressions and Changes*
1. Aesthetic matters (art, architecture, music, literature, houses, cities, parks, interior decorating, furniture, designing).
2. Economic matters (economic stratification, standard of living, commercialization, free enterprise).
3. Family life (husband-wife relationship, wife's role, upbringing of children, marriage, divorce, old people).

4. Crime, law, and social control (law obedience, police, justice, equality).
5. Minority groups (Negroes, Jewish people, ethnic groups, race riots, slums).
6. Politics (*domestic*: interest in political affairs, caliber of politicians, social security, patriotism, meaning of freedom, democracy, the press; *foreign*: aid, NATO, tariffs, United Nations, Russia).
7. Recreation (sports, competition, spare time activities, hobbies, interests, radio, movies, TV, drinking).
8. Religion (church-going, diversity, importance in daily life).
9. Sex-social behavior (dating, rules governing young people's behavior, attitude toward sex, moral standards).
10. Social relations (friendliness, number of friends, depth of friendships, social codes).
11. Social structure (social classes, class consciousness, employer-employee relations).
12. Technology (material comfort, standard of living, technical devices, gadgets).
13. Values and philosophy of life (what are Americans interested in? what do they want to get out of life? what is an "ideal" life to Americans? optimism, rights, freedom, individualism, aggressiveness).
14. In which of the same areas, if any, have your attitudes toward your own country changed since you came to America?

D. *Evaluation of Experience*
1. Do you feel that you are getting out of your stay here what you want? How could it be improved?
2. Have you received the orientation and help you have wanted?
3. Who has been most helpful to you in giving you advice and help (administration, teachers, fellow students, friends).
4. Has your income been adequate? If not, how much more would you need?
5. Do you feel that your progress in language ability has been satisfactory? How could it have been improved?
6. What in particular have you gotten out of your stay here that you could not have gotten by studying at home?
7. Has your educational prestige been influenced by your studies here? How?
8. Have your occupational opportunities been influenced by your stay here? In what direction and how?
9. When you return and somebody comes to you who is going to America to study, what kind of advice would you give him?
10. Which aspects of American life would you like to see transferred back to your own country?
11. When do you expect to return home?

12. Do you expect to come to the U.S. again?
13. What would be your reaction if it were decided right now that you were to remain in the U.S. the rest of your life?
14. After your return home, do you think you will be more likely to defend or criticize America? More or less so than you have done here? Do you think your impressions of America will be the same as they are now?

APPENDIX 2. TEACHER'S RATING FORM

COURSE_____________________

STUDENT'S NAME____ SEMESTER_____________________

INSTRUCTIONS: Under each heading please check the appropriate category. Your answers will be held in complete confidence.

1. *Mastery of English Language*:

_______ Very poor   _______ Good   _______ Excellent

_______ Poor   _______ Very good

2. *Class Participation* (if opportunity was present):

_______ Very little   _______ Average   _______ Very much

_______ Little   _______ Much

3. *Academic Adjustment*:

_______ Very difficult   _______ Average   _______ Very easy

_______ Fairly difficult _______ Fairly easy

4. *Academic Performance in Your Class*:

_______ Poor   _______ Average   _______ Superior

_______ Below average   _______ Above average

5. *Rate of Academic Improvement*:

_______ Very slow   _______ Average   _______ Very rapid

_______ Fairly slow   _______ Fairly rapid

6. *Responsibility* (assignments, appointments):

_______ Very poor   _______ Good   _______ Excellent

_______ Poor   _______ Very good

7. *Sociability*:

_______ Very shy   _______ Neutral   _______ Very outgoing

_______ Rather shy   _______ Rather outgoing

8. *Estimate of Mental Ability* (in comparison with other students):

_______ Low   _______ Average   _______ Superior

_______ Below average   _______ Above average

APPENDIX 3. ADVISER'S QUESTIONNAIRE

STUDENT'S NAME_______________________________________ SEMESTER______________

1. To what extent has this student sought your advice? (Check one)

________ Very seldom   ________ Occasionally   ________ Very often

________ Seldom   ________ Often

2. On what types of problems has this student sought your advice? (Check the appropriate categories)

________ Academic program   ________ Career opportunities

________ Changing courses   ________ Matters concerning visa

________ Grades   ________ Financial matters

________ Research   ________ Housing

________ Fellowships and Assistantships   ________ Personal matters

Others: (Specify) ____

____

3. To what extent has this student followed your advice? (Check one)

________ Never   ________ Most of the time

________ Seldom   ________ Always

4. What have been this student's chief academic difficulties?

____

____

____

____

5. What are some of your impressions of this student?

____

____

____

____

YOUR ANSWERS WILL BE HELD IN STRICT CONFIDENCE

APPENDIX 4. EXCERPTS FROM INTERVIEWS

Since the results of this study were based largely on data from interviews with the forty Scandinavian students, the reader may find it helpful to examine for himself samples of the interview materials. The interviews were all recorded and transcribed verbatim. Each student was interviewed at least four times: as soon after arrival as possible, several weeks after enrolling at the university, several months after entering the university, and again just before he left for home. In these interviews we tried to get information about the student's preconceptions about the United States, his first experiences and impressions, his subsequent experiences and impressions, and his predeparture evaluations of his experience here.

The transcribed interviews run from 60 to 200 pages in length and vary in richness. To present a single interview in its entirety would take considerable space, and no single interview would adequately reflect the nature of the responses of the group. We also believe that to present a single interview would violate the promises of anonymity made to each student — it would be difficult to mask the identity of the informant, at least from other students in the group. Consequently the interview materials presented are excerpts that illustrate the nature of the students' responses to four parts of the interview.

The first excerpt is from an interview with a student who had been in Madison only a few weeks and deals primarily with his preconceptions about the United States. The second is from an interview with another student and pertains to his early experiences and impressions. The third excerpt is concerned principally with another student's subsequent impressions. The final excerpt consists of passages from still another student's final evaluation of his experiences in the United States. The students' nationality and other identifying information has been deleted from all of the excerpts.

SOME PRECONCEPTIONS

Could you tell me about what made you decide to come to study in the United States?

Well, the main thing was to study abroad. First, I had thought of going to Great Britain, because I also wanted to improve my English. Then I applied for different scholarships. I knew I couldn't afford to go to America without help; but then I got this scholarship, so I could come here. I was very happy about this because I expected the opportunities for study here would be broader than in British universities so I could take some work outside my field which I wanted.

Could you tell me what you knew or expected about American university work before you came? The educational system here, the standard of education, the degree of specialization, credits, teachers, and facilities?

Well, looking back, I must say I didn't know much. The main thing I didn't know was the division into undergraduate and graduate work and then this credit system. I got some catalogs and read them and it gave me a pretty good idea, but, you see, these catalogs were written for American students and it seems they assumed you knew some of the basic things. I read as much as I could about this credit system because a fellow I met who had been over here told me it was very important in your work. It's still difficult, though, to understand how the credit system works until you are actually here and see it.

What were some of your ideas as to what going to school here would be like before you came over?

Oh, every so often you saw a movie or pictures in magazines of campuses and university life. It usually looked like fun — not too serious — more on the social line than at home. The buildings and surroundings always looked very nice — and so did the co-eds! It probably gave me a general idea although I realized that it may not be typical. I probably expected teacher-student relations to be more free than at home, but not as free as I found them. This impression I think I also got from movies. Somehow I knew of these true-false kind of exams they have here. I guess I heard that from people who had been over here before I came.

From what you knew before you came here, at what level in the university did you feel you would fit in?

I couldn't quite tell — just from reading the catalogs; but I figured I would be prepared to begin at the junior level, depending on how well I would get along with my English. It's hard to tell beforehand, because a required class in history at the sophomore level may be very advanced or very elementary, you can't tell from a catalog alone. Now that I have seen the system first hand, I think that if you have done well in Gymnasium at home, you should be able to do work at the junior level without difficulty. Of course, the universities here don't all see it that way, I guess, because some of my friends have had difficulty in getting credit for their work at home. It's a difficult problem and you almost have to evaluate each case individually because the language problem is important too, especially in the fields where you have a lot of reading to do.

Before you came, what sort of ideas did you think Americans had of Scandinavians? What did you think they expected a Scandinavian to be like?

Tall and blond! I probably didn't give it much thought. I knew that

Wisconsin was an area of Scandinavian settlement and I'm sure I expected that Scandinavians were well liked and respected — not much different from Americans generally.

Did you have any idea as to how prestige was determined in an American school?

No, not much. That is another thing I didn't give much thought. I probably expected it to be quite similar to home, but I think there are important differences. This whole matter of being socially active and "popular" — it isn't nearly as important at home.

Before you came, how do you think you would have described a typical American?

Ohh — I would probably have characterized him as being quite concerned with the material world — not intellectually inclined — as being unconventional and quite loud in his speech and way of dressing. Those are just general ideas; after all I had seen enough Americans to realize that there were great differences among them.

Where or how do you think you got these impressions?

I think mostly that's the way the typical American was described and pictured in papers and magazines and to some extent it was the same impression you got of the tourists you saw around hotels and places of interest and also the American soldiers after the war. Then again there were the American students at the universities at home, they seemed to be quite different — almost opposite. They dressed very simply — almost sloppily, so it is hard to generalize.

We have talked about American education and American people. Before you came what were your ideas about American family life, and recreation?

Well, again my ideas were very general, but from movies and newspapers I think I got the idea that the family was less stable here — that there were many divorces. About vacations and spare time activities I had the impression that Americans liked to travel — by car and that there was much emphasis on certain kinds of sports which attracted large numbers of people — that many of these sports were half-way professional where the players were paid to play and that there was lots of advertising and money involved. I didn't expect the individual noncompetitive sports to rank very high in popularity although I knew America produced good sportsmen from the results of the Olympics; but here again my ideas were very general and vague.

How about religion in America?

I knew practically nothing about this—only from an occasional newspaper report about some very strange sects. I think I expected more diversity than at home, but not nearly as much religious activity as I found. It has been one of the most surprising things.

What were your impressions at that time about justice and social control, law and order, police and crime and matters of that nature?

Well, there of course the newspapers and movies cover a lot of that. I certainly didn't believe that Chicago was filled with gangsters as I might have heard as a child, but you couldn't avoid getting the impression that the crime rate was high in certain places at least. Then you heard a lot about riots of various kinds but it was not easy to determine why these riots took place. More recently you have heard a lot about corruption sometimes involving the police force — so in general I had the impression that there was more dishonesty and crime than, for example, at home and in many other countries. The most difficult to understand were these race riots and the whole Negro-white problem which were always covered very extensively in the news. It was a very negative part of my feelings toward America. Now I have been here a while and I don't sense this difficulty as much — or maybe it's because I see that the problem is broader. I had no idea before coming about the discrimination against Jewish people — I must say it came as quite a shock because it seemed we were all united against Hitler during the last war and that one of the reasons was his treatment of Jewish people. It has been very disappointing. Also I have studied about the conditions of American Indians since I came here, that is another thing I never expected — that America would have permitted such deplorable conditions to arise and exist. It is very discouraging because, you know, during and after the war we felt very close to the Americans against the Nazi tyranny and inhumanity. I think maybe these things have shaken my faith in some of the programs of aid and assistance which America has carried out since the war. You somehow came to wonder about the intentions — that they are purely humanitarian. Maybe I'll change my mind on some of these matters. I can begin to see, for example, that this Jewish problem is perhaps not a one-sided discrimination. It may be that Jewish people want to be a group by themselves. It's an interesting problem and maybe I'll have different ideas when we talk later on. But I guess this wasn't what you asked about.

That's all right. What ideas did you have about economic life in the United States before you came?

Yah, there is something I forgot to mention before. I remember the papers showing pictures of student riots — these "panty-raids" as they were called. That seemed very strange. I think it was another reason why it was difficult to know about what university life was like here. I must say it seemed more like what one might expect of high school students. Perhaps it gave some idea of the degree of maturity of the students, I don't really remember what I concluded from these reports if anything. — Well, you asked about economic things. There you could hardly avoid getting an impression from magazines and movies and the proverbial "rich uncle in America." It was quite obvious that the movies — the houses and furnishings and so on — didn't give a true picture

of the average American home. Also, the magazines you could buy —
Life and *Time* and so on — had lots of very beautiful pictures of houses
and cars and appliances — it seemed almost unbelievable. I certainly
thought their advertising was very good — very appealing. Perhaps I
can summarize it by saying that almost all products that were made in
America we thought of as being of high quality. Of course this was also
influenced by the war — you remember these German army trucks with
gas generators on them that burned wood and synthetic rubber tires —
and compare them with the American-made army trucks that arrived
— powerful gasoline engines and heavy rubber tires. It was clear to me
that the United States was a country with very rich resources and a
bustling economy. I don't think I had much of an idea about the poor
people — the slums in New York or Chicago that are worse than anything I had seen, certainly worse than anything we have at home.

SOME FIRST IMPRESSIONS

You arrived in New York by boat, is that right?

Yes, and it was very hot! It had been cold at home so I wore heavy
clothes.

How long did you stay in New York?

Only one day. As I said, it was very hot and uncomfortable and I
didn't think New York was a good place to get to know America. Also,
it costs a lot of money to stay there.

*What are some of the things you did in New York? How did you get
around? How did you find places — hotel, places to eat and so on?*

Well, some people from the Institute of International Education met
me and one of them called a hotel and got a room for me. Also, a friend
of mine from —— was at the pier. He was on his way home and he knew
I was coming on this boat.

Did you expect him to be there?

No, I didn't, but we went around together in New York.

*Do you remember talking to any Americans during your stay in New
York?*

Well, I went to buy some lighter clothes. They tried to sell me more
than I wanted!

Had you expected them to try to sell you more than you asked for?

I think so, but not so much. The striking thing about it was that they
talked in a freer tone than we do at home — you know, putting their
hand on your shoulder and so on as though we had known each other
since birth!

What were some of the other things you did in New York City?

I went and saw a show at Radio City, but other than that I didn't
do too much because it was too hot to walk around a lot.

*How about the city itself — the buildings and streets and the people
in the streets?*

Well, of course some of the buildings were impressive by their size, but in general I think I had expected things to be better looking than they were. You can see big buildings next to small ones and parts are added on to buildings with little concern for the total effect. But that's in the city itself — outside in the suburbs you see many beautiful homes and structures. Also New York City was more dirty than I had thought; people seem to throw paper and things around and it isn't cleaned up as well. In general I don't think there is as much emphasis on keeping things clean. In hotels you can find the windows and tables quite dusty. Chicago especially I thought was quite dirty; but maybe it's the climate. It's much drier and more windy so perhaps it's harder to keep things clean.

You mentioned Chicago — how did you get to Chicago?

By bus — it was the cheapest way.

Could you tell me about your bus trip?

Well, it was a long trip — I don't know . . .

Did you talk to anyone on the bus?

Yah, people were very talkative — a little too much! . . . They mostly asked questions . . . "How do you like America?" "Are you going back?" and so on.

From their questions could you tell anything about them?

Yes, I think so. In general I don't think they were very bright. Their ideas about my country were quite strange. They seemed to think it was some backward place and that I would be foolish to think of ever going back!

Did you ask them any questions?

You know, we don't speak too much to strangers like on a bus. It isn't polite to ask too personal questions. Americans don't seem to mind. Now I'm beginning to get more used to it, but in the beginning I must say I disliked it.

How about the places you stopped on the way to Chicago — the rest stops?

Well, I didn't eat too much. The places we stopped didn't seem very clean. Also I wasn't used to these places where you all sit on stools at the same counter all pressed together. I like to eat at a table, so I mostly bought some fruit to eat. Also it was very hot.

How long did you stay in Chicago?

Just a couple of days. You know, I'm used to fresh air and the outdoors, and I guess I don't like big cities, but Chicago, too, was hot and dirty. I stayed in a hotel overnight and the next day I went and saw some relatives.

Had you planned on stopping over in Chicago?

No, but I had the time and I guess I longed to speak my own language again, so I called these relatives. . . . The next day I took the bus again, and, you know, I attended this 6-week session at —— University, so I took the bus to ——. On the way I was mostly interested in seeing the farms. I saw corn for the first time and the different breeds of animals.

Where did you stay in ——?

I stayed in a dormitory along with some of the others who were at this conference and some other people. I didn't get too much out of the lectures because my English was not quite good enough for the new terminology, but I learned some English and I made some good contacts with people in my field.

Living in a dormitory must have been new to you.

Yah, have you ever been in military service? We were three of us in this one room. One thing that was striking was the separation between the sexes. You know, at home you can invite other students to your room — including girl students. I think these rules here are the reason they have these riots where boys break into girls' dormitories and steal their underwear. This would be impossible at home because we are more used to each other.

Had you heard about these raids before coming over here?

Yes, we used to read about them in the papers. We had a lot of fun over them. My friends at home used to tease me and say they would be watching the papers for pictures of me! — It seemed very silly.

Who did you spend your spare time with while you were in ——?

Oh, I met some other Scandinavians. They were regular students there. I went to their rooms at night, we played cards, talked and drank beer. It was the first time I saw a basement apartment — it was rather a sad situation. We spent a good deal of time together, but I would say I spent about as much time with Americans, mostly those who attended the conference.

What did you think of the other Americans you associated with?

Oh, they were very nice, very friendly.

You have been at the University several weeks now. Could you tell me about how things are going?

Well, I think the courses I'm taking are very good. The teachers are very good and interested in their work. They organize their work well. — I think the relationship between teachers here and the students is more free than at home; I like that.

Anything else about your courses?

Only that I don't like these true-false examinations they use here. I do not think these tests give a correct idea of how well the student understands the material. It's much more important to know the basic principles, I think.

I also like my adviser. He is very friendly and helpful. When I first came he looked over my record and sent me to talk to several professors to see how much credit I should get for this or that course at home. They were helpful too. In fact I got more credits than I had expected which was very nice because I could finish up sooner that way. I don't think their evaluation was unfair though because I am not having any trouble at all with the courses I am taking.

How about the other students in your classes? How do they impress you?

It is hard to say, because they are so different; some are good and some not so good. I don't think their high school preparation is very good, not as good as the gymnasium. Especially in mathematics. Even some of the best students are weak in mathematics. I asked a high school student who worked in the lab about his high school education. He was number two in his class, but he knew very little foreign language and the history he had learned was almost all American history, the same with geography. He was quite mixed up on the Scandinavian countries.

What have you been doing in your spare time? Who do you go around with?

Well, sometimes I go for a cup of coffee with some of the American students in the department, but not too often. When I go some place evenings or weekends, it is almost always with the other Scandinavians. It's easier and we understand each other better, you know; it is more relaxing. After a long day's work you don't necessarily want to strain your mind with more new things — and talking.

What are some of the places you have gone?

Oh, one time I went to church; that was quite different. The service itself was much like at home, but, you know, they collected money right in the church! I also saw some small envelopes at each seat where you could either put money in or write how much you wanted to have deducted from your pledge or something. You would write your name and the amount. You know, I must say I didn't like it very much. I was reminded of the quotation: "Don't let your left hand know what your right hand is doing!" — Then when the service was over and we walked out, the minister stood at the door; he saw we were new, and he shook hands with us which would hardly happen at home. It was nice, I think. He was very friendly.

What else have you done in your spare time? Have you taken part in any of the activities around campus?

No, not much. You know, the main thing is that I pay attention to my work so I can finish up before my money runs out! — Sometimes when the weather is nice I go for a walk along the lake. You can observe a lot about American students' ways of making love! — I don't quite understand their moral standards here; they seem to be enforced from outside rules rather than based on the person's own conscience. They have all these rules here about when girls must be in at night and so on — maybe these regulations are the reason why you can find them necking and making love in public. They have no other opportunity. At home, you know, the universities don't try to regulate the students' lives, but of course the students are younger here, so maybe it's necessary. However, I think things would be better if they gave the students more freedom and more responsibility for their own morals.

SOME SUBSEQUENT IMPRESSIONS

You will remember that at our first session last fall I asked you about your opinions of various characteristics of America and American people. Now you have been here almost 10 months. I would like to find out what your present opinions are about some of these same matters. Would you tell me, first, about your ideas of American education? What do you think of the American educational system in general and about the University here in particular — the standards, the teaching methods and classroom procedures, professors, students and so on?

Well, first of all, it seems that the longer I stay here the more I find that I don't know! In the beginning I thought I had a pretty clear idea about everything, but then I discover all kinds of exceptions and things I didn't see or understand before. As far as the educational standards, it is hard to tell because there seems to be quite a difference from one field of study to another. In my own field, I would say the standards here are about the same as at home, but the result is different. The education you get here is much more practical than at home; it looks as though the education you get here is aimed more at what you will do with it when you leave — when you go out and earn a living. The training you get at home is more basic and theoretical. . . . About exams and teaching methods, I don't remember what I told you before, but I probably said some nasty things about these quizzes and tests! Now I think I have gotten used to them and I think there is an advantage to having the exams more often than at home where you study two years or more perhaps before you take an exam. The way here makes the students work more evenly throughout their college years. I think the exams are all right. I do feel that students here are treated less like grown-ups than at home — you don't really feel like a grown-up person here who is interested in the school subject itself; you are watched more and checked on more, and sometimes you come to feel that you go to school to learn what the University expects you to learn, not what you want to learn. . . . I don't know. With so many students maybe it's necessary to have it that way, and especially because many of the American students don't seem as mature as students at home of the same age. . . . It's really hard to compare because, on the other hand, I find that the Americans seem to speak up and say what they think more freely than many young people at home, at least on everyday matters — which may be a sign of independence and maturity — or maybe it is just because they have been brought up that way what with the more free relationship between parents and children and teachers and students, which I like very much.

110

If five or ten years from now you had your own firm and were to hire a person in your field of work, would you prefer to hire a person with an American education or with Scandinavian training?

Well — I think I would really look for a man with basic training from home — say up to the junior level — and then a couple of years of training here. I think that is a very good combination.

We already touched on the matter of people's interrelations in connection with students and teachers. Do you have more to say about that?

I can say that that is one of the things about this country I have come to like very much — the fact that people from different levels can speak to each other freely; like on this job I had, the boss was very informal and all the workers called him by his first name. I suppose it can be carried to extremes and I'm not sure that there is always as much friendliness behind it as you would expect from all these expressions and gestures, but it still breaks the ice and makes people feel good and I think that is nice. — You know, Americans are very friendly when you first meet them and in the beginning I liked it very much and was quite taken in by it; but later on I began to feel that it isn't always as meaningful as you would think from the words used and I came to dislike it some. Now I look at it differently — almost as a technique, and I think in many ways it is a good one; it is a good way for people to get to know each other more quickly — not like at home where it may take a long time before you start asking any personal questions — so I have come to like it more again but for a different reason than before. If there was a way in between, where you could be more informal and free and easy with strangers and yet preserve some of the — what do you call it — genuineness, yah — that would be the ideal.

What are your impressions of American art and architecture, kultur, you might say, American aesthetic values and how people here express them in their surroundings?

Well, I have had some of a professional interest in the design of homes, you might say. When it comes to the average house being built, I would say there isn't much art left — it is almost all science and much of that is economic science — how you can build a house with so and so many square feet for so and so much money. There are many clever ideas which are being used in this type of construction that I would like to adopt. On the other hand, these economic factors have resulted in very standardized architecture — you drive through some of these new housing developments and you see one picture window facing the street after the other, each with a table lamp in the middle. But it is nice that people can have their own homes. At home we try to solve the housing problems by large attractive apartment buildings; it doesn't create as much of a traffic problem for commuters that way. I guess there are advantages in both ways. As far as interest in cultural things, I don't think the average American shows as much active interest as people at home, I mean reading books and going to concerts and so on. Certainly the kind of TV programs they show don't indicate a great demand for culture — it's almost all entertainment and pretty flat at that. But here again it is very hard to generalize because you sometimes meet some people who are very interested in some form of art and may be quite good at playing an instrument or painting or something.

You have already spoken of some aspects of American economic life. What other observations have you made in this area?

Oh, of course I have discovered that not all Americans are millionaires! It certainly seems to me that most people here who want to work can make a good living, and I think the average American works hard — many carry part-time jobs besides their regular jobs. If anything, I would say that my visit over here has strengthened my faith in private enterprise, but I still think this country could learn a lot from us as far as social legislation goes.

I know you have visited several American homes during your stay. What are some of your ideas about American family life?

I think families here seem happy. The parents seem to take a lot of interest in their children and do a lot for them — perhaps sometimes even too much. In the beginning I often thought kids around here seemed rowdy and impolite and I figured they were spoiled from home. I have changed my idea on that somewhat; I think it is just that children here are brought up to express themselves more freely to their parents and other adults than kids at home. I remember at home when we had guests, we kids usually had to eat in the kitchen. Over here the children seem to be more a part of the activities and I like that. Of course you have this teen-age problems and delinquency which doesn't seem to be nearly as bad at home; I don't know why that is, except as I remember when I was that age we were too darned busy to get into trouble.

How about the relationship between husband and wife in American families?

Yah, you see the husband here sharing in the household chores quite a bit, but that is beginning to be quite common at home too, at least among younger couples, so I don't think there is too much difference. On the whole, the American wife no doubt has more influence than at home, but it is changing there, as I say — for better or for worse! I like the American way, though, if it isn't carried too far.

You have already touched on young people's behavior. During your stay you have mostly been around young people — students. What are some of your impressions of them — what they like to do in their spare time, their ideas and ideals and their behavior in relation to the opposite sex?

Oh, boy — there is a lot you can say about that — I think I told you quite a bit about that last time we talked and I think I have about the same impressions now. I still think much of the behavior you see around on campus is childish behavior — there is so much emphasis on having fun — and fun usually means that the more people the better and the more activity and noise the better. You seldom see one, two or a few students out walking or hiking. Then, their dating system seems quite strange and unnatural and, of course, their necking and kissing in public is quite revolting. — Altogether, I don't like this aspect very much, although I have come to see some of the reasons for it — it seems that there are so many restrictions put on young students about what they can do and cannot do and when they must be in at night and so on, that they are almost forced to this public lovemaking. I don't think it is of their own choice. Also, you have all this emphasis on being popular — on who is elected to what office and how many organizations you belong to, sometimes that seems to be more important than the organization itself and what it is trying to do. About this dating and going out with girls — this Danish friend of mine told me about going out with an American girl, and when they came back to the door of where she lived he said "Goodnight," and she said, "Aren't you going to kiss me?" — which is typical, I think. These expressions of love and affection have become meaningless — just something you do. Or else it was so she could tell her friends that she had kissed a boy, which would no doubt add to her popularity, I don't know.

Have you attended any religious services or affairs while you have been here?

No, I haven't. I haven't been too interested in that, but I received quite a few letters or invitations from different churches in the beginning — maybe that was why I didn't go! You know, we like to keep our religion a private or personal thing.

Do you have any impressions of American religious life — the role of the church in the lives of Americans, and what religion means to them?

Oh, well, you see all the different churches and it seems that a lot of people go there — families with all their children, all dressed up. It seems more like a happy thing than at home, which is all right. You know, at home it is quite a solemn affair. Of course, I have my radio, and you hear a lot of religious broadcasts. Also, they seem to get religion mixed into so many different things — just yesterday I listened to this new song where the girl prays to God to make her boyfriend love her. It seems very strange and it certainly wouldn't be heard on the radio at home. It would be — sacrilege. I have the feeling that there isn't too much depth to religion here — although I have no real way of telling. Maybe it is because it is commercialized with the advertising and the collection of money. Somehow you don't associate that with true religion. — I have nothing really against religious life here — I think it is a person's private affair — and in some ways I like the American way better, where the whole thing seems less heavy and solemn than at home.

What else have you been listening to on your radio?

Oh, I hear music — mostly the university station, and then the news. I like the university station better than the other stations — with all their advertisements about soap and hair tonic and what have you — even the political parties advertise their candidates, which seems quite strange.

What are your opinions on how news is reported, both in radio and newspapers?

I think it is often very subjective, and then you have these comments on the news events that are really loaded! Usually it is someone who is mad at all the money this country spends on foreign countries — how it is wasted and how bad the communists are and so on — very much dramatized and only half true — I don't see how it can be allowed that a public communication broadcasts such nonsense. I know it is paid for by private money but it is public in the sense it reaches everyone. It certainly is not flattering to the American people that they can't judge for themselves but have to be fed that kind of stuff. Some Americans don't seem to see that it is to their own benefit to help some of the underdeveloped countries and help rebuild Western Europe. They help build up their own defense. My home is only about a half hour flying time from Russian air bases, so in case of war we will get the worst of it, and if we can't defend ourselves, the Russians will be so much closer to the U.S., so it's for their own good to have strong allies, but some people don't see that here, they don't have much vision when it comes to political things — and that goes for their own domestic politics — they are not well informed, or very interested for that matter — only when it affects themselves directly. Perhaps you can't blame them — the country is so big they couldn't begin to keep up with everything, and the sources of information on matters of public interest are often poor. Take something like *Reader's Digest* — the way they popularize important problems, but maybe this wasn't what you asked about.

It is very interesting. What else have you done in your spare time than listen to the radio?

Oh, I've taken walks; every evening before I go to bed I take a walk for about a mile, to keep myself in some sort of shape. There isn't much you can do here of sports, it seems, of individual sports, it's almost all team sports and organized in clubs. I've missed that some. Also to go away for a weekend out in the open, in the mountains and hills like we used to at home, where you can enjoy nature and get exercise without having to be on a team and play some game for competition and get points and be graded or rated and all that. . . . I went to one football game, but I didn't get too much out of it, I didn't understand the rules anyway, I was almost more interested in the crowd and its reactions — very enthusiastic. It was almost frightening. Then I have gone with [another Scandinavian student] who has a car on small trips and one time we went down to Chicago.

What did you see and do in Chicago?

Well, we saw this Science Museum which was very interesting, and we also drove through the slums — very depressing, very.

Was this a Negro district?

Yah, mostly, and also other people with darker skin. I don't know what they were. They didn't speak English, but I couldn't tell what — maybe Spanish.

What are your impressions now of race problems and minority group problems in America?

Well, as I told you before, I was very surprised to find that it isn't only a problem with Negroes — there are many other groups of people who have bad conditions to live in. But the newspapers at home write only about the Negro problem. And the prejudice against Jews was very shocking to me, of course, and still is. . . . But I think I have come to understand the whole thing more, and I'm beginning to think that if we had a large group of Negroes living in a big city at home, if the same kind of problem wouldn't develop — I don't know. It's a difficult problem. But the Jewish problem was new to me, and I'm still puzzled — because they don't stand out — at least not to me, although by now I have learned to recognize Jewish names that I wasn't aware of before. . . . It's a very complex problem.

How would you describe your reactions to America in general at this point?

That's very hard to do . . . about as hard as to know what to say when people ask: How do you like it here? — which they all do! And they all expect the same answer! — I would say, first, that I am very sympathetic to this country, at least to the American people and to many things you find here — but, you see, it's hard to generalize. I like the Americans very much — they are friendly and informal, which I like. Some of them are quite narrow-minded but some are not. I can certainly say that I understand them better — I know more what they mean when they say something — which I didn't in the beginning so well, I can see now. I am certainly grateful for this experience and I would like to come back for a visit sometime. I'm also going to enjoy reading about this country in the news and so on when I get home, because I will have more background for understanding what goes on. I also think that I will perhaps be even more favorable to America when I get home, because I will forget about some of the small things that frustrate you while you are here — trying to work hard and under pressure and with little money to spend and many nice things to spend it on!

SOME FINAL EVALUATIONS

While you have been here, what are some of the things you have missed about your own country?

Oh, nothing much — well, of course, you miss your family and home life. You have no home life here, of course, no private life. But that hasn't been too serious — you are too busy for that. Oh, maybe at Christmas time and other holidays you miss the traditions a bit.

Take your spare time — have there been any things you have wanted to do that you haven't been able to do?

I haven't had much spare time! Yes, I've missed some the opportunity to get outdoors more — I mean out in the open country — skiing or hiking. You know, it's hard when you don't have a car to get around much. Also, it seems it isn't so common here — to go away for a weekend to someplace — like a lake or in the hills where you enjoy nature and live simply and relax. — But as I said, I haven't had too much time either.

Would you say that you have been able to be with the kind of people you have wanted to be with over here? Are you satisfied with your social life here?

Oh, I guess so. Well, maybe not quite — again, the time has been the main thing. I would have liked to be with the Americans a bit more — now that I look back. My English would have improved by that. But, you know, we aren't too much for joining so many groups and clubs — and much of what goes on is through organizations. But I should say it is my own fault, not the Americans'. I've had many invitations to go to this and that. Also, I would have liked to find out more about people outside the University — I haven't met too many of them. — Yah, I would have liked to be with Americans some more; you know, I've spent most of my spare time with the other Scandinavians — which I regret a little now, but it's a little easier, you see, language and the customs and so on. But I've made friends with some of the Americans too, so generally I'm quite satisfied. After all, you can't do everything in one year's time.

Thinking about your school work here — are you satisfied with what you have gotten out of your stay?

In general, I would say I'm very satisfied. I think I've gotten a lot out of it and that my education here will be of great help in the future. Yes, I'm very satisfied with that. Of course, there are some minor things. I've wished that I could have taken some more elective courses that I have become interested in — related to my field but not really in my field; but then I wouldn't have finished in time and my money would have run out.

Once you get home and start looking for work, how do you think your training here will affect your career opportunities?

Oh, I would say it should help a great deal — that I have been here.

This is a well-known university in my field at home, you know, and also that you have studied abroad should help — it broadens your outlook I think and that should be considered too; also your English should be better as a result. So I would say it is definitely an advantage. Of course, I don't know for sure if my future employers are going to look at it that way, but I think they should, at least!

You mention a broader outlook as a result of your stay — could you elaborate more on that?

What was that —?

You said your outlook has been broadened by your stay here. Could you explain that more?

Well, you see different ways — different ways of doing things. You aren't so tied to only the way you do it at home. You come to understand other viewpoints more. Take the Negro problem — I understand that better — I understand better *who* the people are that discriminate against Negroes — it's not all Americans. Also, the American free enterprise system — I can see better now where we can learn from it and what we can't use of it. It's hard to really explain . . .

Would you say that your outlook on your own country has changed as a result of your stay here?

In some ways, yes. First of all, you come to realize that your country is very small in comparison with the rest of the world — you meet many people who hardly know what it is. Also, you come to see that some of the habits or customs at home are really quite silly, and I've become quite disgusted with some of the inefficiency at home in industry and in the government. — On the other side you come to see the value of some of the things we have — we have no slums, for example, and people seem less rushed and frantic — I think we have better high schools — just to mention some things. And then you can begin to speculate about why these differences are there — so I think you have a broader outlook on your own country that way; you don't just take things for granted.

While you have been here, do you feel you have received adequate advice and guidance — both in educational matters and otherwise? Are you satisfied with that aspect of your visit?

Yah, on the whole I'm satisfied; but you know, as I've said before, there are so many new things — it's hard to know what to expect and what to do — where the best place to live is and if this course is going to be too hard or not — and you can't run and ask for help on every little thing — you have to take some chances, I suppose. You learn more that way anyway. So, I haven't asked for too much advice, and therefore I haven't received too much — but enough, I think. I think without doubt I have gotten most of my advice from the other Scandinavians who were here when I came. You see, they have had the same kinds of problems — I haven't gone to the foreign-student adviser much — only this one time about the visa problem.

How about your adviser in your department?

Yes, of course I have talked to him about my course work and he has been very helpful, very much. He helped me plan my whole program of study and I have been very satisfied with that.

When you get home and someone comes to you for advice who is going over here, what would you tell him?

There isn't much you can tell him — he has to find out for himself — you almost have to experience these things to understand them — well, the more practical things — I can tell him how much it costs to live here, for this and that, and where to live and so on, and also, I'm going to tell him about this credit system at the University and tell him to bring some of his school books along so he can show them to professors and get the right credit, because that is very important and a difficult problem, because it's so different and you can very easily lose time and money if you don't get started at the right level, and the universities here aren't going to give him any more credit than he can prove he should have — every school tries to protect itself and its standards, you know. The other things I'm going to just let him come and discover for himself. That's the way you learn the most — to find out for yourself.

If you could do this entire trip over again — start all over again, so to speak — would there be anything you would do differently?

Hum . . . that's hard to say. Well, if I knew what I know now, I wouldn't have worried quite as much about school work. I would also have tried to be together with the Americans more. That's one thing I regret a little. I don't suppose I would have had more money to spend — if I did I would have liked to travel a little — I would have gone to the West Coast — I'm sorry I haven't been able to see some more of this country, because I probably won't come back here again for a long time. Other than that I can't think of anything — I'm satisfied. It's been a very interesting visit and I will always look back on it with a great deal of pleasure.

What would be your reaction if it was decided right now that you were to remain in this country permanently?

Oh, I'm not sure I would like that. I would prefer to go home. But if it had to be, I'm sure I could adjust to it. After all the two countries aren't too different — at least I can't think of another country outside Scandinavia I would rather go — oh, England or Switzerland would be all right too — but I would prefer to live in my own country. I would like to come back here on visits, of course, and maybe someday I will.

APPENDIX 5. DESCRIPTION OF 33 SELECTED VARIABLES

BACKGROUND VARIABLES

Age: Young to old (8 categories). Based on 2-year intervals from ages 18–29 and 5-year intervals from ages 30–40.

Residential background: Rural to urban (8 categories). 8 categories possible because of different sized towns and cities and because almost every student had lived in different places at different times. Based on interview data.

Socioeconomic status: Low to high (10 categories). The categories are in intervals of approximately 10 per cent on the home-country national scale. Based on interview data.

Leadership in home country: Low to high (9 categories). Based especially on extracurricular activities during secondary school and university. Based on interview data.

Academic performance in secondary school: Low to high (10 categories). The categories represent decile standing on grade-point average in graduating class of gymnasium or secondary school. Based on records.

Previous contacts with other cultures: Low to high (10 categories). Prior contacts with the U.S. excluded; intimacy of contact given more weight than duration and scope. Based on interviews.

Previous contacts with the U.S.: Low to high (10 categories). Personal contacts with Americans such as tourists, soldiers abroad, students at European universities, and relatives, as well as contacts through mass media. Based on interviews.

Prearrival impressions: Unfavorable to favorable (8 categories). Information obtained in retrospect but as soon after arrival as possible. Based on interviews.

English-language facility: Low to high (9 categories). Includes comprehension and vocabulary. Categorization done independently by the interviewer and by the person who transcribed the interviews, with high degree of agreement.

Mental ability: Low to high (8 categories). A summarization of the ratings of students by their university teachers rather than a formal assessment of intelligence by standardized tests. Based on Teachers Rating Forms.

PERSONAL ORIENTATION VARIABLES

Political orientation: Liberal to conservative (10 categories). Based upon the students' self-rating on a 10-point scale in comparison with

119

contemporaries at home. Slightly modified on the basis of interviews, material on political behavior, and organizational membership.

Intellectual orientation: Practical to theoretical (10 categories). Categories arranged on a continuum ranging from interest in and concern with the application of knowledge to interest in and concern with the origin and nature of ideas. Based on interviews.

Nationalism: Low to high (9 categories). Information used included organizational membership in the home country, the nature of reasons advanced for desire to return or not return to home country, and opinions on home country domestic and foreign policies. Based on interviews.

Definiteness of career plans: Indefinite to definite (9 categories). The range was from complete uncertainty about location and nature of job wanted to such definiteness that a job had already been secured. Based on interviews.

Purpose of sojourn: Sociocultural to professional-technical (10 categories). Ranged from primary concern with "interpretation of American culture to fellow countrymen and of native culture to Americans" to exclusive concern with technical training. Based on interviews.

Freedom from preoccupation with home culture: Low to high (8 categories). Differentiation on the basis of interest in news about home country, decoration of room, effort to get films about the home country and to establish contact via radio, membership and activity in local home country organizations, and home country affairs as topic of conversation in informal settings. Based on interviews and participant observation.

PERSONALITY VARIABLES

Social ease: Low to high (10 categories). Ease in novel social situations and ability to initiate and carry on conversations. Based on interviews and participant observation.

Personal flexibility: Low to high (10 categories). Willingness to see a situation from different points of view, the quickness and insight with which a situation was perceived as calling for modification of behavior, and the smoothness and ease with which the modification was carried out. Based on interviews and participant observation.

Freedom from defensiveness of self: Low to high (10 categories). Based on interview data and participant observation.

Dependency: Low to high (8 categories). Based on interviews, participant observation, and advisers' comments especially in respect to the extent to which the student seemed to depend on others in making decisions about academic and personal matters.

Personal adjustment: Low to high (7 categories). Based on interviews, participant observation, and advisers' comments on adequacy of self-perception, nervousness, frustrations, and acceptance by others.

ACADEMIC AND SOCIAL SITUATION VARIABLES

Guidance: Low to high (9 categories). Formal and informal; guidance sought in both academic and nonacademic matters combined. Based on interview data and advisers' questionnaires.

Academic prestige loss: Low to high (8 categories). The range is from feelings of great loss to feelings of some gain in academic prestige as a result of enrollment in the university, credit transfer, and recognition given for past accomplishments. Based on interviews.

Financial support: Low to high (10 categories). Although annual figures were obtained, the actual amount of money was viewed in relation to need: A would receive a higher position than B if their amounts of financial support were the same, but A was single and B supported a family. Based on interview data.

Freedom from frustrations: Low to high (9 categories). Frustrations about language, finances, national loyalty, family matters, occupational and career plans, immigration and visa problems, military service, housing, and academic matters such as grades, requirements, university regulations, and degrees. Based on interview data.

Arrival impressions: Unfavorable to favorable (10 categories). Responses to questions about various aspects of American life and culture were coded on a 5-point scale and these were summarized; the 10 categories represent approximately equal intervals of summary scores. Based on interview data.

Length of sojourn: Short to long (10 categories). Length of time spent in the U.S. by the time of the last interview. The average length was approximately 16 months.

OUTCOME VARIABLES

Participation: Low to high (10 categories). Composite rating based on portion of spare time spent in the company of Americans; extent of contact with the American community (churches, sports, homes, industries, and commercial recreation); extent of dating; and extent of activity in campus organizations and events (other than foreign student activities). Based on interview data and participant observation.

Academic adjustment: Poor to good (7 categories). Those at the favorable extreme accepted the new norms, adjusted easily, and performed well; those at the other extreme rejected the new norms, refused to change, and generally had academic difficulties. Based on interview data and teachers' and advisers' comments.

Final impressions: Unfavorable to favorable (10 categories). Based on rated interview responses, summarized for 15 content areas of American life and culture.

Change in impressions: Less favorable to more favorable (10 categories). Change between the first and the last interviews, which were separated by an average of 9 months. Based on rated interview responses summarized for 15 content areas of American life and culture.

Attitude toward transfer of U.S. features: Less favorable to more favorable (10 categories). "What features, if any, of American life would you like to see transferred back to your own country?" The kinds of features mentioned varied greatly. The content, type, and extent of their transfer recommendations all entered into the ratings. Based on interview data.

Satisfaction with sojourn: Low to high (8 categories). Whether the student felt that sojourn objectives had been accomplished and his general expression of satisfaction with his visit. Based on interview data.

NOTES

Chapter 1. The Background of the Study

[1] Guy S. Metraux, *Exchange of Persons: The Evolution of Cross-Cultural Education*, New York: Social Science Research Council, June, 1952, Pamphlet 9.

[2] Committee on Educational Interchange Policy, *The Goals of Student Exchange: An Analysis of Goals of Programs for Foreign Students*, New York: Institute of International Education, January, 1955.

[3] For further discussion of this research program see Ralph L. Beals' foreword to this volume. Also see Wendell C. Bennett, "Research in Cross-Cultural Education," *Items*, 1952, 6, 3–6; M. Brewster Smith and Joseph B. Casagrande, "The Cross-Cultural Education Projects: Progress Report," *Items*, 1953, 7, 26–32; M. Brewster Smith, "A Research Program on Educational Exchange," *News Bulletin* (Institute of International Education), 1954, 29 (No. 8), 2–6; and M. Brewster Smith, "Report on the Work of the Committee on Cross-Cultural Education," *Items*, 1958, 12, 40–42.

[4] Other published volumes in this series of studies of cross-cultural education include John and Ruth Useem, *The Western-Educated Man in India: A Study of his Social Roles and Influence* (New York: Dryden Press, 1955); Franklin D. Scott, *The American Experience of Swedish Students: Retrospect and Aftermath* (Minneapolis: University of Minnesota Press, 1956); Richard D. Lambert and Marvin Bressler, *Indian Students on An American Campus* (Minneapolis: University of Minnesota Press, 1956); Ralph L. Beals and Norman D. Humphrey, *No Frontier to Learning: The Mexican Student in the United States* (Minneapolis: University of Minnesota Press, 1957); John W. Bennett, Herbert Passin, and Robert K. McKnight, *In Search of Identity: The Japanese Overseas Scholar in America and Japan* (Minneapolis: University of Minnesota Press, 1958); and Richard T. Morris, *The Two-Way Mirror: National Status in Foreign Students' Adjustment* (Minneapolis: University of Minnesota Press, 1960).

[5] Institute of International Education, *Education for One World: Annual Census of Foreign Students in Institutions of Higher Education in the United States*, 1952–53 and 1953–54.

[6] A second series of studies designed to test propositions emerging from the exploratory studies is being sponsored by the Committee on Cross-Cultural Education, Social Science Research Council. See Ralph L. Beals' foreword to this volume and the materials cited in notes 3 and 4.

[7] For many years Norway has furnished half or more of the total number of Scandinavian students studying in the United States. See *Education for One World*, 1952–53, pp. 45–46.

[8] Eight of the forty students were here as recipients of the Viking Scholarship founded by Thomas E. Brittingham, Jr., a well-known benefactor of the University of Wisconsin. This scholarship enables promising young Scandinavians to attend the university for one year during which they are encouraged especially to participate extensively in student life and activities.

[9] See *Education for One World*, 1952–54, Table II.

[10] The interview guide was based on a preliminary list of variables relevant to the study of cross-cultural education which was developed by Herbert Hyman of Columbia University. The guide prepared by the staff of the Scandinavian project was used with appropriate modifications in the studies of Indian, Japanese, and Mexican students.

[11] In order to assure uniformity and objectivity in the coding and rating of interview responses, fifteen of the early interviews were coded independently by the interviewer

and two other members of the research team. All differences were checked and agreement reached. The remaining interviews were coded independently by the interviewer and one other team member. In those few instances where significant disagreement occurred another team member was asked to resolve the difference. In this way a high degree of reliability was developed in the coding operation.

Chapter 2. Academic Experiences and Adjustment

[1] American Association of Collegiate Registrars and Admissions Officers, *Report of Scandinavian Study Tour: A Preliminary Study of the Educational Systems of Denmark, Finland, Iceland, Norway, and Sweden*. World Education Series, March, 1959. Prepared by Eunice Chapman. For a description of the situation in Norway, see Einar Haugen, *A Study of the Norwegian University Entrance Examinations or "Antium" Degree with Notes on the University of Wisconsin Policy for Foreign Students*. (3rd revised edition, Madison: University of Wisconsin, 1951). For a brief description of the Swedish educational system see Scott, *op. cit.*, pp. 8–16.

[2] Facilities for training engineers are particularly limited; this is especially true in Norway. Consequently, many very able students must go abroad for engineering training. Several of the students in the sample could not gain admission to technological institutes in the Scandinavian countries because of the severe competition for places but did outstanding work here.

[3] See Folke Schmidt, *Vidgat Tillträde Till Högre Studier* (Statens Offentliga Utredningar, 1952) pp. 10–22, and Bertil Ostergren (Editor) *Higher Education in Sweden* (Stockholm: Swedish Institute, 1952) p. 39. The situation in the other Scandinavian countries is quite similar to that in Sweden.

[4] *U.S. Census of Population, 1950*: Vol. II. Characteristics of the Population, Part 49, Wisconsin, Chapter 13. Washington: U.S. Government Printing Office, 1952, p. 96.

[5] In fact, there seems to be less of a tendency for Scandinavian students to form a student community of their own than for students whose cultural backgrounds are quite dissimilar to the American students'. For an interesting description of a foreign student community, see Lambert and Bressler, *op. cit.*, pp. 23–28.

[6] The figures on grade-point averages were obtained from Joseph L. Lins, Director of Student Personnel Statistics and Studies, University of Wisconsin.

[7] Franklin D. Scott, *op. cit.*, Ch. V., found that the career opportunities of returned Swedish students had been enhanced as a result of their study in the United States.

Chapter 3. Social Experiences and Adjustment

[1] Franklin D. Scott, *op. cit.*, p. 7.

[2] Again, the students were probably evaluating sojourn experiences on the basis of home culture norms. Organizations and clubs play a relatively minor role in the lives of young Scandinavians.

[3] For an interesting comparison see typology for Japanese students developed by John W. Bennett, Herbert Passin, and Robert K. McKnight, *op. cit.*, pp. 110–113.

Chapter 4. Impressions of American Culture and Personality

[1] Similar results were found for Norwegian Fulbright scholars. See Sverre Lysgaard, "Adjustment in a Foreign Society: Norwegian Fulbright Grantees Visiting the United States," *International Social Science Bulletin*, 7 (Spring, 1955), 45–51.

Chapter 5. Relationships of Selected Variables to Outcomes

[1] The use of this statistic may be challenged because the usual assumptions of the product-moment coefficient of correlation are not completely met by the data. Ordinarily one of the non-parametric measures of correlation, such as Spearman's rho or Kendall's

tau, would be more appropriate. (See M. G. Kendall, *Rank Correlation Methods*, London: Charles Griffin & Co., Ltd., 1948.) In the early stages of the analysis, these methods were considered but were not adopted because it soon became apparent that it was not possible to assign ranks to the forty students on a number of the variables. In other instances, where it seemed possible to rank the students, the reliability of the rankings made by two or more judges was rather low. On the other hand, independent ratings involving assignment of each student to an ordered category on a given variable could be done with high interjudge agreement when the number of categories was not large (from 7 to 10 categories). Consequently, the following procedure was used: each student was placed in that category which the judges agreed was most closely descriptive of his behavior for each of the 33 variables; these categories were assigned discrete numbers (1, 2, 3, . . . n) ordering them along the continuum under consideration; and these numbers (rather than ranks, scores or other measures) became the raw material for the computation of the correlation coefficients. For the relatively crude purposes to which the measure of association is put in this exploratory study, this procedure has the advantage that it is easily carried out on IBM equipment and provides a widely understood coefficient; however, inferences based on the results must be made with caution because the mathematical assumptions underlying the product-moment coefficient of correlation are not fully met.

[2] In exploratory studies it is common to set an arbitrary standard which will permit retention of variables for discussion whenever the coefficient is high enough to account for an appreciable amount of the total variance. No formal convention exists but the standard of .30 is commonly used with samples of this size (40 cases). In instances where all of the assumptions of the product-moment coefficient of correlation are met, it can be shown that the total variance which can be predicted by the knowledge that the correlation coefficient is .30 is 9 per cent (the square of the correlation coefficient). Moreover, a correlation coefficient of .30 would be significant at the .05 level for samples of this size if tests of significance were applied.

It should be understood by the reader that the coefficients themselves provide no basis for causal inferences. They merely give an indication of the extent of the relationship between two variables. The nature of the variables involved and observations of the students' behavior are the only guides to causal direction in the relationships explored. For these reasons, as well as those mentioned in the previous footnote, interpretation of the correlations is made with caution and is intended to be suggestive rather than final.

[3] Reflecting the typically rational and pragmatic Scandinavian approach to culture change they chose quite specific features of the American culture. Their responses were often accompanied by qualifications aimed at avoiding transplantation of aspects which "are all right in America but won't fit at home." Besides technological improvements and conveniences such as automobiles, appliances, and various gadgets, the features most frequently mentioned for adoption were ease and informality in social relations, freedom of the economy from governmental control, equality and sharing of household duties between husband and wife, and separation of church and state. For further discussion of Scandinavian attitudes on this topic, see Franklin D. Scott, *op. cit.*, pp. 4–5.

Chapter 6. Conclusions and Implications

[1] M. Brewster Smith has discussed a number of practical implications of the findings of studies of cross-cultural education in "Some Features of Foreign Student Adjustment," *Journal of Higher Education*, 26 (May, 1955), 231–241.

[2] Since the writers first called attention to this developmental trend in the adjustment of Scandinavian students (William H. Sewell, Richard T. Morris, and Oluf M. Davidsen, "Scandinavian Students' Images of the United States," *The Annals*, 295 (September, 1954), 134–135) similar results have been reported for other foreign student groups. See Ralph L. Beals and Norman D. Humphrey, *op. cit.*, pp. 50–53, and Sverre Lysgaard, *op. cit.*, pp. 45–51.

³ For a careful study of such programs see Jeanne Watson and Ronald Lippitt, *Learning Across Cultures: A Study of Germans Visiting America*. Ann Arbor: Institute of Social Research, University of Michigan, 1955.

⁴ For further evidence on this point see Richard D. Lambert and Marvin Bressler, *op. cit.*, Ch. 5 and "The Sensitive Area Complex: A Contribution to the Theory of Guided Culture Contact," *American Journal of Sociology*, 60 (May, 1955), 583–592; Ralph L. Beals and Norman D. Humphrey, *op. cit.*, Chs. 10–11; Cora Du Bois, *Foreign Students and Their Education in the United States*, Washington, D.C., American Council on Education, 1956, Chs. 8 and 10; M. Brewster Smith, "Some Features of Foreign Student Adjustment," *Journal of Higher Education*, 26 (May, 1955), 236–237; and Richard T. Morris, "National Status and Attitudes of Foreign Students," *Journal of Social Issues*, 12 (Spring, 1956), 20–25.

⁵ For a discussion of research in cross-cultural education see M. Brewster Smith, "A Perspective for Further Research on Cross-Cultural Education," *Journal of Social Issues*, 12 (Spring, 1956), 56–68, and "Cross-Cultural Education as a Research Area," *Journal of Social Issues*, 12 (Spring, 1956), 3–8.

⁶ Some interesting evidence on this point based on observations and interviews with Swedish returnees is given by Franklin D. Scott, *op. cit.*, Ch. V.

BIBLIOGRAPHY

Barghoorn, Frederick C., "The Soviet Image of the United States: A Deliberately Distorted Image," *The Annals*, 295(1954), 42–51.

Beals, Ralph L., "The Mexican Student Views the United States," *The Annals*, 295(1954), 108–115.

———, and Norman D. Humphrey, *No Frontier to Learning: The Mexican Student in the United States*. Minneapolis: University of Minnesota Press, 1957.

Bennett, John W., "Cross-Cultural Education Research and the Study of National Acculturation," in *Some Uses of Anthropology: Theoretical and Applied*. Washington: Washington Anthropological Society, 1956.

———, "Misunderstandings in Communication between Japanese Students and Americans," *Social Problems*, 3(1956), 243–256.

———, Herbert Passin, and Robert K. McKnight, "The Japanese Overseas Student," *Institute of International Education News Bulletin*, 31(1956), 30–34.

———, *In Search of Identity: The Japanese Overseas Scholar in America and Japan*. Minneapolis: University of Minnesota Press, 1958.

Bennett, Wendell C., "Research in Cross-Cultural Education," *Items*, 6(1952), 3–6.

Brodersen, Arvid, "Themes in the Interpretation of America by Prominent Visitors from Abroad," *The Annals*, 295(1954), 21–32.

Buchanan, William, "How Others See Us," *The Annals*, 295(1954), 1–11.

Chapman, Eunice, *Report of a Scandinavian Study Tour: A Preliminary Study of the Educational Systems of Denmark, Finland, Iceland, Norway and Sweden*. World Education Series, 1959.

Cherrington, Ben M., "Ten Years After: Ten Years of Intercultural Relations," *Association of American Colleges Bulletin*, (1948), 500–522.

Cieslak, Edward C., *The Foreign Student in American Colleges: A Survey and Evaluation of Administrative Problems and Practices*. Detroit: Wayne University Press, 1955.

Committee on Educational Interchange Policy, *The Goals of Student Exchange: An Analysis of Goals of Programs for Foreign Students*. New York: Institute of International Education, 1955.

Committee on International Exchange of Persons, *Educational Exchanges: Aspects of the American Experience*. Washington: Conference Board of Associated Research Councils, 1956.

Conference on Student Life and Education in the United States. Chicago: University of Chicago Press, 1954.

Cook, Stuart W., and Claire Selltiz, "Some Factors Which Influence The Attitudinal Outcome of Personal Contact," *International Social Science Bulletin*, 7(1955), 51–58.

Denney, Reuel, "How Americans See Themselves: Studies of American National Character," *The Annals*, 295(1954), 12–20.

Du Bois, Cora, "Research in Cross-Cultural Education," *Institute of International Education News Bulletin*, 28(1953), 5–8, 60–64.

———, "The Dominant Value Profile of American Culture," *American Anthropologist*, 57(1955), 1232–1239.

———, *Foreign Students and Higher Education in the United States*. Washington: American Council on Education, 1956.

———, *Handbook on International Study*. New York: Institute of International Education, 1955.

Festinger, Leon, and H. A. Kelly, *Changing Attitudes through Social Contact*. Ann Arbor: Institute for Social Research, University of Michigan, 1951.

Flexner, Abraham, *Universities: American, English, German*. New York: Oxford University Press, 1930.

Forstat, Reisha, "Adjustment Problems of International Students," *Sociology and Social Research*, 36(1951), 25–30.

Freymond, Jacques, "America in European Eyes," *The Annals*, 295(1954), 33–41.

Fulbright, J. William, "Open Doors, Not Iron Curtains," *New York Times Magazine* (August 5, 1951), 18.

Goldsen, Rose K., Edward A. Suchman, and Robin M. Williams, Jr., "Factors Associated with the Development of Cross-Cultural Social Interaction," *Journal of Social Issues*, 12(1956), 26–32.

Goodwin, William F., Jr., "Scandinavia," *Focus*, 5(1955), 1–6.

Haugen, Einar, *A Study of the Norwegian University Entrance Examination or "Artium" Degree with Notes on the University of Wisconsin Policy for Foreign Students* (3rd ed. revised). Madison: University of Wisconsin, 1951.

Humphrey, Norman D., "The Mexican Image of Americans," *The Annals*, 295(1954), 116–125.

Institute of International Education, *Education for One World: Annual Census of Foreign Students in Institutions of Higher Education in the United States*. New York: Institute of International Education, 1949–1954.

———, *The Population Involved in International Education*. New York: Institute of International Education, 1955.

———, *Open Doors: A Report on Three Surveys*. New York: Institute of International Education, 1955.

Kendall, M. G., *Rank Correlation Methods*. London: Charles Griffin & Co., Ltd., 1948.

Kiell, Norman, "Attitudes of Foreign Students," *Journal of Higher Education*, 22(1951).

Knapp, Robert B. (Editor), *Orientation to America for Foreign Exchangees*. Washington: American Council on Education, Series I, Reports on Committees and Conferences, No. 54, 1952.

Lambert, Richard D. (Issue Editor), "America Through Foreign Eyes," *The Annals*, 295(1954).

———, and Marvin Bressler, "Indian Students and the United States: Cross-Cultural Images," *The Annals*, 295(1954), 62–72.

———, "An American Education for Students from India," *Journal of Higher Education*, 26(1955), 125–133.

———, "The Sensitive-Area Complex: A Contribution to the Theory of Guided Culture Contact," *American Journal of Sociology*, 60(1955), 583–592.

———, *Indian Students on an American Campus*. Minneapolis: University of Minnesota Press, 1956.

Leonard, Olen E., and Sheldon G. Lowry, "International Exchange of Persons" in Charles P. Loomis, et al., *Rural Social Systems and Adult Education*. East Lansing: Michigan State College Press, 1953, pp. 244–270.

Lesser, Simon O., and Hollis W. Peter, "Training Foreign Nationals in the United States" in Rensis Likert and Samuel P. Hays, Jr. (Editors), *Some Applications of Behavioral Research*. Basel, Switzerland: UNESCO, 1957, Ch. V.

Lippitt, Ronald, and Jeanne Watson, *Principles and Techniques for Planned Change*. New York: Russell Sage Foundation, 1955.

———, "Some Special Problems of Learning and Teaching Process in Cross-Cultural Education," *International Social Science Bulletin*, 7(1955), 59–65.

Loomis, Charles P., and Edgar Schuler, "Acculturation of Foreign Students in the United States," *Applied Anthropology*, 7(1948), 17–34.

Lysgaard, Sverre, "Adjustment in a Foreign Society: Norwegian Fulbright Grantees Visiting the United States," *International Social Science Bulletin*, 7(1955), 45–51.

McKnight, Robert K., and John W. Bennett, "Liberation or Alienation: The Japanese

Woman Student in America," *International Institute of Education News Bulletin*, 31(1956), 38–53.

McMurry, Ruth E., and Muna Lee, *The Cultural Approach: Another Way in International Relations*. Chapel Hill: University of North Carolina Press, 1947.

Metraux, Guy S., *Exchange of Persons: The Evolution of Cross-Cultural Education*. New York: Social Science Research Council, Pamphlet No. 9, 1952.

Miller, Helen A., "U.S. Government Programs of International Exchange: 1952," *The Educational Record*, (1953), 313–326.

Morris, Richard T., "National Status and Attitudes of Foreign Students," *Journal of Social Issues*, 12(1956), 20–25.

———, *The Two-Way Mirror: National Status in Foreign Students' Adjustment*. Minneapolis: University of Minnesota Press, 1960.

Muhlen, Norbert, "America and American Occupation in German Eyes," *The Annals*, 295(1954), 52–61.

National Association of Foreign Student Advisers, *Handbook for Counselors of Students from Abroad*. Experimental edition. New York: The Association, 1949.

Oestermann, Richard, and Donald E. Neuchterlein, *God's Own Country and Mine: America and Denmark*. Copenhagen: Nyt Nordisk Forlag, 1951.

Olsen, Lionel R., and William E. Kunhart, "Foreign Students' Reactions to American College Life," *Journal of Educational Sociology*, 31(1958), 277–280.

Olsson, Jan Olof, and Margareta Sjögren, *Onkel Sams Stuga*. Stockholm: Bonniers, 1952.

Ostergren, Bertil (Editor), *Higher Education in Sweden*. Stockholm: Swedish Institute, 1952.

Passin, Herbert, and John W. Bennett, "The America-Educated Japanese," (Parts I and II), *The Annals*, 295(1954), 83–107.

Perlmutter, Howard V. "Relations between the Self-Image, the Image of the Foreigner, and the Desire to Live Abroad," *Journal of Psychology*, 38(1954), 131–137.

Political and Economic Planning, *Colonial Students in Britain*. London: Political and Economic Planning Report, 1955.

Pool, Ithiel de Sola, Suzanne Keller, and Raymond A. Bauer, "The Influence of Foreign Travel on Political Attitudes of American Businessmen," *Public Opinion Quarterly*, 20(1956), 161–175.

Peterson, James, and Martin H. Neumeyer, "Problems of Foreign Students," *Sociology and Social Research*, 32(1948), 787–792.

Reigel, O. W., "Residual Effects of Exchange of Persons," *Public Opinion Quarterly*, 17(1953), 319–327.

Riecken, Henry W., *The Volunteer Work Camp: A Psychological Evaluation*. Cambridge, Mass.: Addison-Wesley, 1952.

Robertson, David A., "International Educational Relations of the United States," *Educational Record*, 6(1925), 91–150.

Rose, Arnold M., "Some Consequences of Brief Cultural Contact," *Phylon*, 13(1953), 125–132.

Schmidt, Folke, *Vidgat Tillträde Till Högre Studier*, Statens Offentliga Utredningar, 1952.

Schwantes, Robert S., "Results of Study Abroad: Japanese Students in America, 1865–1885," *School and Society*, 72(1950), 375–376.

Scott, Franklin D., *The United States and Scandinavia*. Cambridge, Mass.: Harvard University Press, 1950.

———, "The Swedish Students' Image of the United States," *The Annals*, 295(1954), 136–145.

———, *The American Experience of Swedish Students: Retrospect and Aftermath*. Minneapolis: University of Minnesota Press, 1956.

Selltiz, Claire, Anna L. Hopson, and Stuart W. Cook, "The Effects of Situational Factors on Personal Interaction between Foreign Students and Americans," *Journal of Social Issues*, 12(1956), 33–44.

Sewell, William H., and Oluf M. Davidsen, "The Adjustment of Scandinavian Students," *Journal of Social Issues*, 12(1956), 9–19.

Sewell, William H., Richard T. Morris, and Oluf M. Davidsen, "Scandinavian Students' Images of the United States: A Study in Cross-Cultural Education," *The Annals*, 295(1954), 126–135.

Shirer, William L., *The Challenge of Scandinavia*. Boston: Little, Brown, 1955.

Simenson, William, and Gilbert Geis, "A Cross-Cultural Study of University Students," *Journal of Higher Education*, 26(1955), 21–25.

Smith, Howard P., "Do Intercultural Experiences Affect Attitudes?" *Journal of Abnormal and Social Psychology*, 51(1955), 469–477.

———, "The Effects of Intercultural Experience: A Follow-up Investigation," *Journal of Abnormal and Social Psychology*, 54(1957), 266–269.

Smith, M. Brewster, "A Research Program on Educational Exchange," *Institute of International Education News Bulletin*, 29(1954), 2–6.

———, "Some Features of Foreign Student Adjustment," *Journal of Higher Education*, 26(1955), 231–241.

———, "Research in the Field of International Education," in *Handbook on International Study*. New York: Institute of International Education, 1955, 235–252.

———, "The Future of International Exchange Programs," *Teachers College Record*, 57(1956), 285–289.

——— (Issue Editor), "Attitudes and Adjustment in Cross-Cultural Contact: Recent Studies of Foreign Students," *Journal of Social Issues*, 12(Spring, 1956).

———, "Cross-Cultural Education as a Research Area," *Journal of Social Issues*, 12(1956), 3–8.

———, "A Perspective for Further Research on Cross-Cultural Education," *Journal of Social Issues*, 12(1956), 56–68.

———, "Report on the Work of The Committee on Cross-Cultural Education," *Items*, 12(1958), 40–42.

———, and J. B. Casagrande, "The Cross-Cultural Education Projects: Progress Report," *Items*, 7(1953), 26–32.

Snyder, Harold E., "Neglected Aspects of International Cultural Relations," *School and Society*, 74(1951), 321–325.

Taba, Hilda, *Cultural Attitudes and International Understanding: An Evaluation of an International Study Tour*. New York: Institute of International Education, 1953.

UNESCO, *Study Abroad: International Handbook of Fellowships, Scholarships, Educational Exchange 1952–53*. Paris: UNESCO, 1953.

United States Advisory Commission on Educational Exchange, *Fourteenth Semi-annual Report on Educational Exchange Activities*, U.S. Congress, House of Representatives, 84th Congress, 1st Session, House Document No. 219, Washington: U.S. Government Printing Office, 1955.

United States Bureau of the Census, *U.S. Census of Population: 1950*. Vol. II, *Characteristics of the Population*, Part 49, Wisconsin, Chapter 13. Washington: U. S. Government Printing Office, 1952.

United States Congress, House Committee on Appropriations, *Hearings, Department of State Appropriation Bill for 1950*, U.S. Congress, 81st Congress, 1st Session, 1949, Washington: U.S. Government Printing Office, 1949.

———, *Public Law 402 (United States Information and Educational Act)*, U.S. Congress, 80th Congress, 2nd Session, 1948, Washington: U.S. Government Printing Office, 1948.

———, *Public Law 584 (Fulbright Act)*, U.S. Congress, 79th Congress, 2nd Session, 1946, Washington: U.S. Government Printing Office, 1946.

United States Department of State, "Educational Exchange under the Fulbright Act in 1954," *Department of State Bulletin*, (1955), 232–243.

United States Educational Commission in the United Kingdom, *The Fifth Annual Report on the Fulbright Program in the United Kingdom and Colonial Territories, 1949–1954*. London: Millbrook Press, 1955.

BIBLIOGRAPHY

Useem, John, and Ruth H. Useem, *The Western-Educated Man in India*. New York: Dryden Press, 1955.

Useem, Ruth Hill, and John Useem, "Images of the United States and Britain Held by Foreign-Educated Indians," *The Annals*, 295(1954), 73–82.

Watson, Jeanne, and Ronald Lippitt, *Learning Across Cultures: A Study of Germans Visiting America*. Ann Arbor: Institute of Social Research, University of Michigan, 1955.

Wheeler, W. R., H. H. King, and A. B. Davidson, *The Foreign Student in America*. New York: Association Press, 1925.

Williams, Herbert H., *Foreign Study for Syrians: A Guide to a Long Range Program*. New York: Institute of International Education, Occasional Paper No. 4, 1953.

Wilson, E. C., and F. Bonilla, "Evaluating Exchange of Persons Programs," *Public Opinion Quarterly*, 19(1955), 20–30.

Wilson, Howard E., *Universities and World Affairs*. New York: Carnegie Endowment for International Peace, 1951.

Wofford, Kate V., *The Workshop Way with Foreign Students: A Report of a Turkish Project in Rural Education*. Gainesville: University of Florida Press, 1954.

Woodyatt, Philip, "We Are So Kind: An American Examines His Country's Attitudes toward 'Foreign Students,'" *International House Quarterly*, 19(1955), 10–15.

Zajonc, Robert B. "Aggressive Attitudes of the 'Stranger' as a Function of Conformity Pressures," *Human Relations*, 5(1952), 205–216.